THERE'S A DOG IN THE HEAVENS!

A UNIVERSE OF CANINE VERSE

by

MARTIN ELSTER

HATS
OFF™

There's a Dog in the Heavens!
A Universe of Canine Verse

Back cover photo by Joseph Zaborowski.

International Standard Book Number: 1-58736-153-1
Library of Congress Card Number: 2002095484

Published by Hats Off Books
610 East Delano Street, Suite 104
Tucson, Arizona 85705
U.S.A.
www.hatsoffbooks.com

To Igor and Nala

PREFACE

Igor and Nala (my motley mutts) must have inspired me. Why else would an otherwise rational person write hundreds of limericks about dogs? When I'd see them sunning themselves, playing (and occasionally fighting) with each other, rolling on grass (or less pleasant substances), chasing a ball (or a squirrel), wagging their tails, gnawing on a bone, or simply watching me with their expressive, mysterious eyes — well, these things would give me ideas. In fact, I had so many "dog-thoughts" filling my mind, it's a wonder I didn't begin eating kibble for breakfast! (Being a vegetarian was the only thing that stopped me.)

You are about to em-bark on a journey through a uni-verse of limericks (and "other-verse") about dogs. You'll encounter an assortment of rather curious canine characters along the way — like a Yorkie from New York-y who's almost as light as a quark-y; a mutt who can open doors, write, and draw with a paw; a dog from Nantucket who gets her head stuck in a bucket; or a musical Rottie who listens to Scarlatti. You'll also meet coyotes, dingoes, foxes, African Cape hunting dogs, and giant wolves.

"That's my dog!" you will say. But if you don't have one, some of these poems may inspire you to adopt one (or two or five). Inevitably, you'll come upon a melancholy poem or two ("Adopt Me Please" or "Elegy For Laika"). There are dogs, alas, whose water bowls really are half empty.

I hope you have as much fun reading these poems as I did writing them. Have a ball! (And then throw it for your dog to fetch.)

M. E.

You can learn how a dog fights or plays,
And read tales about heroes and strays,
And more in this book.
So friend, have a look
At the dogs this collection portrays.

DOG DEFINITIONS

A *dog* is someone mean or vile —
A crook who might be put on trial.
Lucky dog: Those words suggest
A person who is charmed or blessed.
A dog's not just one's loyal pal,
But also she's an ugly gal.
A man who dogs you *doggedly*
Pursues or tracks persistently.
The *dog days* are the hottest days
Of summer when the sun's rays blaze.
A book which has its corners worn
Is *dog-eared* (but let's hope not torn).
Ruthless competition is
Dog-eat-dog. Well, that's show biz!
An elementary swimming stroke,
The *dog paddle's* good, though you'll be a slowpoke.
If your dog is lost with no *dog tag*
That really would be quite a drag!
If you let your property go to pot
'Twill *go to the dogs* — like it or not!
"*I must see a man 'bout a dog.* OK?"
What he means is he just wants to get away.
You drank too much? You feel hung over?
Have *the hair of the dog* — but not from Rover!
If you're *in the dog house,* best try to save face,
For you're now in disfavor and much disgrace;
If you don't want to stir up any more trouble,
Let sleeping dogs lie, so your trouble won't be double.
If you're *sick as a dog,* your mutt might lick
Your nose, 'cause he knows you're very sick.
If you're *top dog* in a wrestling bout,
Then you've won the match without a doubt.

It's been a dog's age since I rode my bike
Or been in the woods to take a long hike.
If you feel like being pretentious for Joey,
Then *put on the dog.* Be pompous and showy.
A *hot dog's* a showoff, a shameless fool
Who does dangerous stunts and thinks it's cool.
Now let's be serious. Sirius, the star,
Is the brightest star in the heavens by far!
The *Dog Star* is what astronomers call it;
With telescopes they often eyeball it.
Well, this is as far as this poem must get,
For scores more poems await you yet.

1
DOWN THE RIVER

My dog is now controlling
The direction we are going.
We're in a boat that is afloat.
My dog's the one who's rowing.

We're going down a river.
The breeze gave me a shiver.
He's rowing well, he's really swell!
So I'll give him some liver.

I did but he said, "More!"
Then he simply dropped the oar.
He's now all wet, 'cause my dear pet
Jumped out and swam to shore!

The oar is gone. It sank.
The dog ran up the bank.
What will I do with this canoe?
My mind just draws a blank.

The current's getting faster.
I hope there's no disaster!
Will I survive? Remain alive?
My dog still needs a master!

I think I do recall
A giant waterfall
Just up ahead. I'll soon be dead.
I dread that water wall!

Out of the boat I jumped.
Against a rock I bumped.

I did my best at swimming lest
I'll o'er the falls be dumped.

It was hard to keep from sinking.
H-2-O I started drinking.
I thrashed around — tried reaching ground.
What was my mutt now thinking?

Rushing water's all I hear now.
But what's that coming near now?
Is that a log? No, it's a dog
Swimming in high gear now!

And before I came to harm,
My large canine grabbed my arm.
While the rapids roared, he pulled me toward
The shore (by Fisher's farm).

Though I very nearly drowned,
He no longer fooled around;
For he got me out, and there's no doubt
My dog's a fearless hound!

The boat was lost forever,
Yet my dog thinks he was clever.
We're both now dry. We didn't die,
But never, never, never

Will that dog go on a trip
With me in car or ship.
When I told him so he growled low
And gave my leg a nip!

Since there's nothing I can tell him,
Perhaps I'll simply sell him —
Well, maybe not. 'Twas just a thought —
For I cannot expel him

From my life, 'cause we're together
Just like two birds of a feather;
Though, through thick or thin, from here on in,
I'll keep him on a tether!

2
THE DOG STAR

There's a *dog* in space! Am I delirious?
No! Its eye is a star they call Sirius;
    The brightest by far,
    It's a binary star—
With its unseen companion, mysterious!

The companion is known as "the pup."
Do you think that I just made that up?
    That white dwarf is as small
    As a puppy's toy ball.
If you ask, "Is that true?" I'd say, "Yup!"

3
THE STAR DOG

He sprinted and leaped toward the sun
For Frisbees—he did not drop one!
    A bit of a ham,
    The great mutt Soarin' Sam
The world championship three times had won!

4
FETCHING A STAR

Were my dog to try fetching a star,
He might climb to the roof of my car,
    And then jump up so high—
    He's so agile and spry—
That he may even reach a quasar!

5
THE FIRST IN SPACE

Who was the first in space?
It wasn't the human race.
    It was Laika, a dog,
    Who could snooze like a log,
Or jump up to lick your face!

6
BEAUTY IS MORE THAN FUR DEEP

It's his character, not pedigree,
That counts. Do you with that agree?
    When I see a canine,
    I see not his blood line,
But the way he behaves around me.

7
SIMONE GETS HER DOG BACK

There's this neighborhood dog, a bit thin —
A Shepherd just like Rin Tin Tin.
 He's a little bit shy
 (I don't really know why),
So I gave him a bottle of gin.

He lapped up the drink and got drunk,
And into a slumber he sunk.
 His dream was quite sweet:
 He was back in New Skete
With his very first master, a monk.

But he suddenly woke in a fright.
It was now very dark; it was night.
 He had heard a strange noise:
 A couple of boys
Nearby were engaged in a fight.

Totally sober by now,
He knew that he couldn't allow
 A brawl to take place,
 So he gave them a chase,
Then got hungry and searched for some chow.

He instead found a Chow with long hair
Who was almost as fat as a bear!
 They found some good trash
 Mixed with stale corned beef hash,
But the Chow ate it all. Was that fair?

So the Shepherd took off on his own
And luckily found an old bone.
 He started to paw it
 And happily gnaw it,
But stopped, for it tasted like stone.

He was noticed by someone named Sloan,
Who, without delay, dialed his phone.
    A lady then came,
    Called the Shepherd by name,
And then took the dog straight to Simone,

Who was very ecstatic and glad.
And no longer depressed and as sad
    As the day when her dog
    Disappeared in a fog
And she thought she would surely go mad.

The dog, being gone for two years,
Didn't see his poor master's big tears.
    But now he is back
    In his old home, his pack,
And Simone often strokes his big ears.

The dog now stays close to his master.
He won't even walk too far past 'er.
    He'd defend his Simone,
    Who no more walks alone,
With his life if some hoodlum harassed 'er.

8
ALLIGATORS

If you're near a big Florida lake,
Keep your dog by your side for his sake.
    If he wanders too near
    There's always the fear
That a 'gator will rush out and take!

9
GIVE THEM A CHANCE

Why some dogs are mean is a puzzle.
They really should wear a good muzzle.
    But if given a chance,
    They could learn to enhance
Their most basic desire: to nuzzle.

10
A RACE BETWEEN TWO SPECIES

The dog ran too fast for his master.
He easily galloped right past 'er;
    For he's so well designed,
    And his legs so aligned,
That the sprinter's dog truly outclassed 'er!

11
TRICKED 'ER!

Though he threatened his dog with a club,
She still wouldn't go near the tub;
    When he showed her some liver,
    She thought he'd deliver
The goods, but instead got a scrub!

12
WILL HE NEVER LEARN?

My dog just got sprayed by a skunk!
'Cause sometimes he's truly a "lunk!"
    The smell is so strong!
    It lingers so long.
I wish my dog no longer stunk!

13
THE "BEA GULL"

By the shore lives a colorful Beagle
Who thinks himself ever so regal.
    He sees many birds.
    Though he speaks not their words,
He behaves as if he were a sea gull.

The way he survives on the beach
Is to scavenge whatever's in reach.
    He's a curious sight,
    For his fur is all white.
From the sun even Beagles can bleach!

14
THE AIREDALE

Down the street lives a friendly Airedale
Who's in search of a friendly female.
    His bark is quite loud,
    And though he's quite proud,
He has yet to get any fan mail.

15
WATCH THAT FOX!

A fox ran away with your socks!
He's hiding behind those big rocks.
    If you're eating some fish
    As a little side dish,
Watch out! He'll come back for your lox!

16
A SEEMING CONTRADICTION

My pooches won't swim in the ocean
'Cause the waves are forever in motion;
    And the taste of the salt
    Is a major assault,
Yet they'll play in the sun without lotion!

17
GRAZING

On our way to obedience class,
My dog stopped to munch on some grass.
    Though it made him throw up,
    That did not shake me up,
'Cause, thank God, it did not give him gas!

18
OPPORTUNIST

If your dog does not always abide
By your rules that you sometimes let slide,
    Then you're not quite consistent
    So he'll be persistent
And grab your whole pizza and hide.

19
THEY NEED A HOME

There are too many strays for sure,
Yet all of their souls are pure.
    They're all unique.
    They all just seek
A home where they'll feel secure.

20
SMELLY KELLY

I have a large mutt I call Kelly
Who rolls on some objects so smelly
    That for days she will reek,
    Or even a week,
Yet she wants me to rub her pink belly.

21
AUSTRALIAN DRUMMERS?

What kind of a dog is a dingo?
Do you think he plays rock drums like Ringo?
    Though he scavenges trash,
    He makes no big splash,
For he'll always stay clear of a gringo.

22
DO YOU KNOW WHAT YOUR DOG SMELLS LIKE?

When near my dog's paws what I smell
Is burnt popcorn, I think I could tell.
    His ears smell quite musty,
    His fur rather dusty,
His mouth I won't go near! Oh well.

23
WHAT DID MY DOG ROLL IN?

Though my dog smelled just like a wet rug,
I wanted to give him a hug.
    But when I got close,
    My nose got a dose
Of something so gross I said, "UGH!"

24
HOGGING THE BED

When that doggy gets up on the bed,
He acts like he's made out of lead.
    Though he's really a dog,
    You may think he's a hog,
When there's no space for even your head!

25
IS THE DOG ON THE BED AGAIN?

When I try to roll onto my side,
That doggy will just not abide.
    I'll push and shove her,
    But she'll just go, "GR-R-R,"
And my legs always feel like they're tied!

26
IN A DINER

In a diner where I went to eat,
They served me some grilled doggy meat.
    I, out of ear shot,
    Said, "I'd rather eat snot!
'Cause it's cold," and yelled, "Waiter, reheat!"

27
NO HITTING

Your dog is as loyal as can be;
In thick or thin won't forsake thee.
    So don't hit your dog!
    (Or even a frog.)
If the hitting urge strikes, slap your knee!

28
THE BEST TRICK OF ALL

A mutt who was some Poodle mix
Was arrested for doing weird tricks,
    Like a seal with a ball.
    But the best trick of all,
And what freed him, was giving wet licks!

29
PROGRESS?

There once was a Sheltie named Dew
Who would never roll over on cue.
    He could not do one trick
    Like fetching a stick,
But escaped through a screen—a breakthrough!

30
DOG TAGS

If he has no ID on his collar,
And your dog runs away when you holler,
    Then gets himself lost,
    And in the pound tossed,
They'll fine you much more than a dollar!

31
THEIR PURPOSE IN LIFE

A Pembrokeshire Corgi herds cattle,
A Pit Bull's designed for a battle,
    Sheep dogs herd sheep,
    Show dogs ain't cheap,
And Newfoundlands do the dog paddle.

32
LIKE LASSIE

Siblings Wally and Ollie and Polly
Have a beautiful dog they call Molly.
    Many times she did save
    Those three children. She's brave!
She's exactly like Lassie — by Collie!

33
RED THING

Did you know a dog's tongue perspires?
It's just what their body requires.
    That red thing hangs out,
    It's wet all throughout,
And when licking you, it never tires!

34
A MIND OF HER OWN

I have a strong-willed Finnish Spitz.
When I tell her to come, she just sits.
    When I tell her to stay
    She wanders away,
And I'm now at the end of my wits!

35
AN ARTIST

My dog is so clever and smart
On my rug he created some art.
    His muddy paw prints
    Had such colorful tints —
For an art career, not a bad start!

36
A "DOGGIAN SLIP"

As my fingers plowed through some Beethoven,
My Beagle slipped out for some rovin'.
    When he later came back
    And I gave him a whack—
I mean SNACK!—we felt quite interwoven.

37
HIS NOSE KNOWS

More efficient than any machine,
A dog's nose can detect what's unseen;
    From searching for bombs,
    To finding pompoms,
It's made quite a few smugglers come clean!

38
EAGER TO PLEASE? OR EAGER FOR? ...

On his hind legs my doggy will stand,
Or lie down, sit, or heel on command.
    Is he eager to please?
    Nah. It's the cheese
I so temptingly hold in my hand!

39
YOU CAN NEVER LOSE A BLOODHOUND

From just one drop of sweat on your clothes
A Bloodhound can track you by nose
    For one hundred miles.
    (The thought just beguiles.)
He'll go crazy just smelling your toes!

He can tell the direction you went
If the trail has a fresh enough scent.
    A few sniffs and he's off.
    At his talent, don't scoff!
When tracking, he sure is hell-bent!

40
A LONG HAUL

A tiny Chihuahua, quite small,
On the arm of his owner, quite tall,
    Began losing his grip,
    And started to slip
Straight down. It sure was a long haul!

41
MAYBE HE NEEDS A SEAT BELT

My dog loves to go ride in the car
Whether the trip is a short one or far.
    He hangs halfway out,
    And I haven't a doubt
That one day he'll just land on the tar.

42
INCREDIBLE EARS!

Those sounds that we call ultrasonic,
To the ears of a dog are euphonic.
 For their ears are so keen
 (If they're kept fairly clean)
That the soundscape for them is symphonic!

43
AVALANCHE

A neighborhood dog saved a boy.
The boy who was saved was called Roy.
 The dog led his master
 To the site of disaster,
And pulled out the child with joy!

Roy went to ski down a hill,
But above him was snow that could kill.
 The snow was packed loose
 On the hill with some moose,
And the scene was yet quiet and still.

But a great snowy avalanche waited,
And as soon as the loose snow vibrated,
 It came tumbling with speed —
 God did not intercede —
For Nature cannot be evaded!

Though the avalanche started quite slow,
It began to get heavy with snow.
 Above to the right,
 A horrible sight,
And the boy could not even yell, "NO!"

For just then the snow buried the child.
It hit him with force and then piled
    On top and around him.
    The white did surround him,
And the feeling of cold was not mild!

He lay there and started to freeze—
His hands and his feet and his skis.
    He could not move a muscle
    Or hear a small rustle;
Could he see, he would see roots of trees.

But somebody saw this take place.
Against the clock they now did race.
    The dog used his nose,
    And before the boy froze,
They dug him right out of that place.

Though the child experienced hell,
He recovered and now is quite well.
    He thanks that great mutt
    For saving his butt,
And admires his keen sense of smell.

44
THE KEY TO TRAINING

Are you asking me if you should hit?
I'd say, "Sure, if you want to get bit!"
    For I think the key
    To dog training, for me,
Is rewards, lots of praise, and my wit!

45
A BETTER APPROACH TO ADOPTING A DOG

Are puppy mills all that humane?
Some folks would say they're insane!
    If you want to pay more
    Then buy at the store,
But that dog may be sick or in pain.

Why not just visit the pound —
Where you're certain to find one that's sound?
    Though you wouldn't pay much,
    Your dog would be such
A good friend — his love will have no bound!

46
OUTSIDE THE STORE

If your dog waits outside of a store,
While you're shopping, for him it's a bore.
    So do not delay,
    For he might start to stray —
And just hope he is still at the door!

47
PLAYING ALONG TOO LONG

He makes rhythms while water he laps.
So get your drum, make your own taps.
    And when your dog eats,
    Go make up some beats,
If you tire just take some dog-naps.

48
ADVICE

If you keep your dog locked in a cage,
He'll eventually show you some rage.
    So give him a walk.
    And then a "pet-talk,"
Then write this advice on a page.

49
NO ACCOUNTING FOR MUSICAL TASTE

When I put on some Franz Joseph Haydn
My doggy will somewhere be hidin'.
    While Benjamin Britten
    Will leave him just sittin',
Stravinsky will make his ears widen.

50
REYNARD THE TRICKSTER

The red fox, like a cat, stalks and pounces
On a rodent that weighs a few ounces.
    His cunning's well known.
    He goes it alone.
In a farmer's dream, this fox he trounces!

51
BEING WET

If you don't rub your dog with a towel,
When he's wet from the rain, he will scowl.
    And I'll make you a bet
    That your dog, being wet,
Will just shake and your furniture foul.

52
THREE-LEGGED

A dog who was missing a leg
Did just fine without needing a peg.
    On him you could count
    That your leg he would mount
If you'd not pay him heed when he'd beg.

53
POISE

I was walking my dog down a trail
When we noticed a small cottontail.
    Though my dog kept his poise,
    He let out a faint noise
'Cause my foot was on top of his nail.

54
A MYTH

Can your older dog learn a new trick?
Do you think he is really that thick?
    Don't believe in that myth
    'Cause that mutt you live with
For some pizza can get very quick!

55
NO, BUT THEY KNOW

Are dogs from some higher dimension?
Well, they sure have a keen comprehension
    Of our feelings, unseen,
    If we're mad or serene.
They're aware of our every intention.

56
PAY ATTENTION, JACK!

An athletic, young mongrel named Fang
Tried his best to fetch a boomerang;
    But that thing came right back
    To his master named Jack,
Who, while watching Fang, felt a big bang!

57
AN UNUSUAL DOGGY

A doggy with barely a hair,
The Hairless is virtually bare.
    He'll keep you quite warm
    In a cold winter storm
If your bed he is willing to share.

58
A BIKE RIDE WITH ROVER

If you go for a bike ride with Rover,
Make sure he does not tip you over.
    Be sure that he heels
    To one side of your wheels,
And make sure you don't run Rover over!

59
CHARLEY
To Rose Darby and her dog, Charley

There's this little Fox Terrier, Charley
Who won't run from the sound of a Harley.
    Though he'll try to go hump
    Every dog's rump,
He's quite friendly and never gets snarly.

60
CAN'T HOLD IT THAT LONG

If you're away from your house for too long,
With your dog inside, that would be wrong.
    For he may leave a present
    You would not think too pleasant
When you walk in and smell something strong.

61
BISCUITS FROM GEORGE

There's a smallish and quaint laundromat
In West Hartford where folks come to chat.
    Their dogs come to gorge
    On biscuits from George,
But Lisa says, "Don't bring your cat!"

62
KONG

There's a toy made of rubber, quite strong —
A popular one called the Kong.
    If you stuff it with cheese,
    It your dog will appease,
And he'll happily play all day long.

63
PLAIN COMMON SENSE

Do you often get nervous and tense
'Cause your yard doesn't have a good fence?
    You're afraid he might roam,
    Won't stay close to his home?
Well, then get one! — it's plain common sense!

64
BEST FRIENDS

I can see a distinct similarity
Between you and your dog — not a rarity:
    You're both large and lanky
    And frequently cranky;
Most obvious? Your solidarity.

65
ABUSED

Does your dog from your raised hand recoil?
Perhaps he can sense your blood boil.
    His teeth are now bared,
    For he's often been scared.
To retrain him you may need to toil.

He acts as though he doesn't hear you.
Why, the poor thing won't even get near you —
    'Cause you've yelled at him often.
    Perhaps if you soften
Your voice, he would no longer fear you.

66
A GHOST, 1864[*]

John Simpson[1], a Confederate spy
Was sentenced by Panton[2] to die.
    His final request,
    While under arrest,
Was to see his dog, Pete[3], and say bye.

But as guards led John Simpson him away,
Panton's soldiers his mutt they did slay
    With their hard rifle butts
    (Which did not take much guts)
And did not for poor Pete even pray.

Next morning while lashed to the post[4],
Simpson thought that he saw his dog's ghost.
    He looked at his feet
    And said, "Why, it's Pete!"
Panton stared and went pale, quite engrossed.

At the prisoner's feet he did stare.
What he saw there sure gave him a scare!
    A vaporous fog
    In the shape of a dog —
A dog that was made of thin air!

Transfixed, Panton couldn't say, "Fire!"
Tried twice but then lost his desire.
    "Execution deferred!"
    Was his stammered last word —
And so Simpson's life did not expire.

Said John, after being set free,
"It was Pete at my feet I did see!
    My good buddy, concerned,

From dog heaven returned.
My true, loyal mutt had saved me!"

*_Based on a story in_ **Mutts: America's Dogs** _(Kilcommons &_
Capuzzo, 1996)
[1] _Private John Simpson_
[2] _Union Colonel Panton_
[3] _A black-and-white mongrel_
[4] _Shooting post_

67
NOT WHAT HE EXPECTED

Thought the fellow who stumbled upon it,
'Tis a valuable tome! I will pawn it.
    But when he took a look
    Inside of that book
He cried, "Dog poems? Worthless, doggone it!"

68
TRULY OBSESSED

Have you heard of this really cool Rottie
Who's aware of his powerful body?
    Though he's quite easy going,
    His taste is mind-blowing,
For he loves to eat _naan_ and _chapati_.

Indian food he likes best.
He will gobble up _dosas_ with zest.
    He craves all those spices
    And exotic rices
Which fennel seeds help him digest.

From his diet he's clearly digressed,
Since his dog food he will not ingest.
    Though there is some protein
    In his choice of cuisine,
Would you not say this dog is obsessed?

69
AN OBEDIENT SCHNAUZER

Do you know this large black female Schnauzer
Who often will nip at your trouser?
    The squirrels she'll chase,
    Or bark in your face,
But only when her master allows 'er.

70
IF HE NABS THAT BUNNY
IT WON'T BE FUNNY

My Beagle's been chasing this rabbit
For days. It's become quite a habit.
    That bunny is quick,
    But my dog could get sick
From its flesh should he actually nab it.

71
SYMBIOSIS

Sometimes my dogs make me mad
When they do something I think is bad,
   (Like chew up my clothes,
   Or eat all my "O's")
But I quickly forgive and am glad,

'Cause my canines can cure my neurosis.
It's a human and dog symbiosis.
   They're man's closest friend,
   So we should commend
The dogs in our lives that engross us.

72
CRAZY NEIGHBORS

Their car alarms drive me insane!
They go off all the time — it's a pain —
   Without rhyme or reason,
   Regardless of season.
Yet "Fido" barks once, they complain!

73
BO
To Troy Roccanello and his dog, Bo

An American Bulldog named Bo
Is as white as some new-fallen snow.
   With the dogs he plays hard
   In the neighborhood yard,
And when running he sure isn't slow!

You really should be on your toes
When he chases the dogs and the crows.
    Jump out of his way!
    Don't just stand there and pray
When he misses you just by a nose.

Sometimes the pace really quickens
When the dogs run around like some chickens.
    If you don't look around
    Then you may just get downed,
And your thigh bone will hurt like the dickens!

When Bo whizzes by you'll go, "WHOA!"
'Cause you know he could give quite a blow.
    For he'll often not see
    Where you happen to be,
So move quick or your knee he may throw!

74
NOT ON THE BUS

They won't let my dog on the bus.
I don't understand all the fuss.
    For they'd make much more money
    (Is that thought so funny?)
If the bus driver charged both of us.

75
DOGS IN WINTER

Does your dog always sleep in the yard?
Chained in winter, that could be quite hard.
    If your dog has short hair

Then she won't have a prayer.
For her health you must have some regard.

The snow can be cold for her toes,
And frostbite can get on her nose.
    So bring her inside.
    Your warm home she's denied?
Then at least do not hardship impose.

In nature a dog would just dig
A den, and she'd make it quite big.
    But chaining your mutt
    Right on to that hut,
She'll feel like she's some guinea pig.

So provide her with adequate shelter
So frozen rain pellets won't pelt 'er.
    Increase her food ration,
    And show her compassion.
(In summer make sure she'll not swelter.)

Provide water by breaking the ice.
Each day break the ice at least twice.
    And get her a sweater
    To make her feel better,
And that is my moral advice.

76
PRIVATE CHIPS: WAR HERO

The most famous of war dogs was who?
Private Chips, Shepherd mix, World War Two.
    A mind of his own,
    He did it alone:
Captured six men with guns — it is true!

On Sicily's shores, wanting rest,
Chip's men found a fort; empty, they guessed.

But machine guns were there,
Which gave them a scare
When Chips ran in first, self-possessed.

A machine gun they heard blast away,
And were sure on the floor their dog lay.
　　Then heard no sound at all
　　Come through that thick wall,
So they charged in without much delay.

What they saw was that Chips (you may quote)
Had his teeth on the machine gunner's throat!
　　The Italians, quite scared,
　　Had their arms raised, lives spared,
So this story ends on a high note.

The capturing of that gun nest
In Sicily made Chips the best
　　War hero ever;
　　Though wounded, was clever,
And the men he watched over were blessed!

Though awarded the Silver Star,
He got no Purple Heart for his scar.
　　Did that make him bitter?
　　Well, that little critter
Bit Dwight Eisenhower. "Har har!"

Note: Based on a story in **Mutts: America's Dogs** *(Kilcommons & Capuzzo, 1996).*

77

"I WOULDN'T SEND MY COCKROACH BY AIR."

— Phyllis Wright, former vice president,
Humane Society of the United States

Transporting your doggy by air
Is not wise, for he may not get there.
    It's much safer by car
    No matter how far
'Cause the airlines do not really care.

Your dog hears those jet engines blare,
And they really could give him a scare.
    When the air's hot and sticky
    Your dog will feel icky.
To him it is quite a nightmare.

He's left in the plane's cargo hold
For hours if it's hot or it's cold.
    He'll try to get out
    'Cause he knows he'll pass out.
The fatalities, they are untold.

Your dog has not much air in there.
But they'll tell you he's fine; they will swear.
    He'll sit on the ramp
    When it's hot, cold, or damp,
So you must for your dog say a prayer.

Dogs' brains have been literally cooked
When their cries have been all overlooked
    By the "well-meaning" staff.
    But it's really a laugh
When they've not at the dogs even looked.

Airlines do pay token fines,
But they really should have warning signs.
    They'll tell you he's well,

But for him it is hell!
And there's no one to hear your dog's whines.

Many canines have actually died
While having their aeroplane ride.
    (Is it safe in the skies?
    Don't believe in such lies!)
And those dogs were, no doubt, terrified.

78

SPRING

To Joe and Joan Harrison Ceo and their late dog, Spring
(Violist, Harpist, and Vocalist, respectively)

A musical doggy named Spring
Loved to hear Mrs. Ceo's harp ring;
    But the fiddle Joe played
    Made poor Spring so dismayed
That she'd howl and virtually sing!

While howling, she'd lift up her chin,
And the Ceos would often join in.
    They'd howl right back,
    They developed a knack,
And produced such a horrible din,

That the neighbors would often complain.
They thought that these folks were insane
    Until one splendid day,
    Last April or May,
When they all brought their dogs and champagne!

Now the whole neighborhood howls!
They wake all the bats and the owls.
    The wolves in the hills
    Even join in for thrills,
But all cease when a single dog growls!

79
WHEN HE'S HOT YOU CAN TELL
AT A GLANCE

Why do you think your dog pants?
Do you think he's a hot dog perchance?
　　His mouth opens wide,
　　His tongue does not hide,
And he surely does not need sweat pants!

80
A CALMING INFLUENCE

Did you know that your doggy can lower
Your blood pressure, make your heart slower?
　　Though you might have some fleas,
　　You'll be much more at ease
The longer that you get to know 'er.

81
VERSATILE CANINES

In Islam despised and eschewed,
In China he's cooked up as food;
　　For some he's a pet,
　　For others a threat,
But for most he's a friend, I'll conclude.

82
BRILLIANT OBSERVATION

There once was a dog from Nantucket
Who got his head stuck in a bucket.
    He couldn't get free,
    And the crowd could just see,
That this doggy was really quite stucket!

83
MANGE

Your poor doggy has sarcoptic mange.
I hope I am out of her range!
    Also called scabies,
    It can infect babies
Or me! — it could make me look strange!

This illness is caused by a mite:
A small tick-like bug that can bite.
    That mite so abuses
    Her skin, it just oozes.
The sight of her gives me a fright!

However, it's quite reassuring
To know that your dog who's enduring
    This suffering can get
    Rid of this yet
Before the disease starts maturing.

From the vet in your town or location
Get some Lymdyp, a good preparation.
    When the dog gets so itchy
    Her skin is all twitchy,
This stuff will ease her agitation.

You can use a shampoo with oatmeal.
It will help your dog's itching, for real.
 And a natural diet
 Is crucial. Go try it!
These things will all help your dog heal.

84
MANGE: FROM THE DOG'S PERSPECTIVE

"This disease has my beauty disguised!
And I fear I will be stigmatized.
 So please cure my skin
 Before it does me in
With that stuff that the vets have devised."

85
THE CYCLONE

A doggy named Clark, left alone,
Became scared when he heard a cyclone.
 He jumped through the screen
 And tried leaving the scene
But got caught and away he was blown.

He was finally dropped to the ground.
Three miles away he was found.
 Though completely unhurt
 When he hit the soft dirt,
The experience did him confound.

From then on when he heard a whirlwind,
The poor dog got so anxious he grinned,
 And hid under the bed,
 Or ran into the shed,
For fear of being gone with the wind.

86
CRUMMY DOG FOOD

The mongrel belonging to Strauss
Was arrested for chasing a grouse.
    But in jail was so good
    They said, "He is no hood,"
And then brought him right back to his house.

But the very next day near his house
Was arrested for catching a mouse.
    But they then did conclude
    That the crummy dog food
That Strauss feeds him means Strauss is a louse.

87
VITAMIN A

One of my dogs loves a carrot.
She'll chew it and eat it, I'll swear it.
    Though she'll eat every piece
    She does not get obese,
And she'd choke before she'd ever share it!

88
A FULL STOMACH

There once was a dog from Nantucket
Who got her head stuck in a bucket.
    She was drinking some water
    When that old pail got 'er
And knew that when freed she'd upchuck it.

89
WHAT WAS THAT NOISE?

There once was a dog from Nantucket
Who got his head stuck in a bucket.
    He heard a loud clang
    And then both his ears rang
'Cause some jerk with a stone had just struck it.

90
AN EXCEPTION

Perhaps more than a husband or wife,
Your doggy can lighten your life;
    But not if the brat's
    Chasing everyone's cats,
And the rest of your town's wildlife!

91
THEY HELPED CIVILIZE US!

Which creature was first on this earth
To sit by our side at the hearth?
    It wasn't a hog
    Or a frog, but a *dog!*
And they do give us our money's worth!

92
OBLIVIOUS MASTER

There once was a dog from Nantucket
Who got her head stuck in a bucket.
    She then heard her master
    Walk blindly right past 'er
And thought, *That was just my bad lucket.*

93
THE DAY I JOINED THE WOLVES

My parents were constantly fighting;
Of my faults they were scolding and chiding.
    So one day last May
    I just ran away,
And encountered a wolf — how exciting!

This big timber wolf on the loose
Came towards me so I yelled, "Vamoose!"
    Scared half to death,
    I just held my breath.
And then I thought, *What is the use?*

He'll eat me for dinner right now.
I felt lots of sweat on my brow.
    But the wolf simply sat.
    Imagine that!
And I could not help but say, "Wow!"

He then looked right into my eyes;
The look in his seemed very wise.
    He lifted a paw,
    Which held me in awe.
My opinion I then did revise.

He now did not seem quite so scary;
He now only looked very hairy.
    And I thought, *You know,*
    A long time ago
Partners we were on the prairie.

Now a whole pack of them came.
They all seemed remarkably tame.
    As I followed them home,
    I created this poem,
Then gave each giant wolf his own name.

Now I am part of their pack.
Of companionship there is no lack.
    We howl at night
    When the full moon is bright.
To my old home, please don't send me back!

94
ONE OF A KIND

Each doggy is one of a kind.
They get along well with mankind.
    They're all unforgettable,
    Also quite pettable.
Petting one helps you unwind.

95
OVERREACTION

Her voice rising more than a notch,
Snarled the woman, "He sniffed at my crotch!"
    She got so upset
    And she made such a threat
That you'd think the dog stole her wristwatch!

96
BEAR

There once was a mongrel named Bear
Who for charm most dogs couldn't compare.
  He always was seen
  With his owner named Jean
Who was young and had really long hair.

One day Bear took off somewhere.
Jean had no clue as to where.
  She did not know that Holly,
  A Shepherd-slash-Collie,
Had lured her good doggy elsewhere.

They were having a "doggy affair,"
But Jean just thought Bear was unfair
  To have left her like that
  At the drop of a hat,
So she cut off her beautiful hair.

She patiently waited and waited.
On his whereabouts she speculated.
  When he didn't return
  There was lots of concern
From Jean's friends, who were all devastated.

Although Jean would at times get quite blue,
She never lost hope cause she knew
  That Bear would come back,
  Return to the "pack,"
Though just when she did not have a clue.

When, at last, Bear came back to his Jean
He received quite a hug from the teen.
  Jean was so happy
  She got sort of sappy
And called up her girlfriend, Irene.

"Bear is back! Isn't that great?
I think he was out on a date.
    With whom and just where
    I don't know and don't care,
'Cause from now on I'm latching my gate!"

97
LIKE FIREFLIES

I lost track of my dogs at twilight,
So I got each a Pet Tracker light.
    (They attach to their collars,
    Cost just a few dollars.)
My dogs look like fireflies at night.

98
YUM-YUM!

Are hot dogs for dogs a hot item?
Those long fatty things sure delight 'em!
    It's a good training aid,
    For dogs tailor-made.
Into small pieces cut 'em — divide 'em.

From a distance you call, "Sammie, COME!"
He smells hot dog pieces, yum-yum!
    He runs towards you full speed
    'Cause he sure wants to feed
On those morsels — that dog's no dumdum!

99
AN EXCELLENT MEMORY

A gal with a Volkswagen bug
Years ago gave my dog a big hug.
    So now when one nears,
    He perks up his ears
And runs after that loud "chug-a-lug."

100
MAX

There once was a mongrel named Max
Who liked to hang out by the tracks.
    He'd sit on the rail
    And wag his big tail
When he'd hear the train's clickity-clacks.

He'd barely move out of the way.
If you saw this, your hair would turn gray!
    It was kind of a game,
    But you cannot him blame
When he didn't quite make it one day.

It was winter with ice on the ground.
Old and deaf now, did not hear the sound
    Of the big train approaching
    Which on him was encroaching,
And the poor dog did not look around.

He was sleeping when he suddenly sensed
The train almost on him and tensed,
    But slipped on the ice,
    So paid a big price,
For his master should've had that dog fenced.

101
A RIDDLE

Which doggy's tongue is blue-black?
His ancestry goes quite far back:
    One-fifty B.C.
    From the Han Dynasty.
This polar dog once was a snack.

102
THE STORY OF SAM

There lives an old mongrel named Sam
Who was always just told to go scram.
    When he came for some bread
    They just kicked him instead,
For these folks just did not give a damn.

The town he lived in had no heart.
The folks did no kindness impart.
    He had not one friend;
    For himself he did fend,
Yet that dog was incredibly smart.

Then one day he saw a boy fall
Into an icy pond during a squall.
    He bravely jumped in
    And saved that boy's skin,
And since then he's been adored by all!

Is there to this story a lesson?
Perhaps here's a moral worth stressin':
    A poor homeless stray
    That folks chased away,
Overnight was a hero—a blessin'!

103
ALAS, SHE WILL NOT EVER COME

A very large litter of ten
Are waiting for food in their den.
    Their mother's away
    Hunting for prey,
Her returning they do not know when.

Alas, she will not ever come,
'Cause for "sport" she was killed by a bum.
    That wolf tried to run
    From the fool with the gun,
But she did from his bullet succumb.

So I think that man should be taken
And roasted till he is charred bacon,
    'Cause that jerk doesn't care
    How those cubs will now fare,
And the thought of it leaves my soul achin'.

104
MY GREAT PYRENEES

Though my Great Pyrenees chases geese,
The vet said she's much too obese.
    Her white fur is quite shaggy,
    Her tail's very waggy.
To me she's a great masterpiece!

She's not only loyal and smart,
She pulls children around in a cart.
    She's as strong as an ox
    And as smart as a fox,
Though her weight really is off the chart!

105
POCKET DOG

If you'd rather just carry than walk it,
Your Chihuahua can fit in your pocket;
    But if there is a hole
    While you're taking your stroll
Then the slide down your pant leg might shock it!

106
JELL-O

When I bring my dogs into the park
They go sniffing around and they mark.
    The snow becomes yellow.
    It looks like it's Jell-o.
But no one's yet made a remark.

107
IN VANDERBILT PARK

I'm in Vanderbilt Park viewing plants
When a dog comes and pees on my pants!
    That very rude hound
    Then scratched the ground
And sauntered away with a prance!

108
THE STRANGE WOLFARANER

There once was a tan Wolfaraner
Who lived in a very large manor.
 Every day she went out
 And just roamed all about.
From the sun she got tanner and tanner.

Each time she would wander aroun'
She'd come back looking more and more brown.
 Her owner would stare
 At her darkening hair
And from sheer disbelief would just frown.

Her fur got so dark it was black
Except for one spot on her back.
 This spot was light green.
 This could not be foreseen,
And her owner was taken aback.

What do you think he then did?
The owner just wanted to rid
 Himself of that strange
 Dog for some change,
So he gave her to his neighbor named Sid.

Now Sid was an artist, quite smart.
He thought that this dog could be art.
 So he painted her blue
 Of an interesting hue,
But "The Green Spot" — did not touch that part.

The two of them toured round the world.
Great compliments everyone hurled.
 The "Green Spot" was hot!
 They all loved that spot,
But between her back legs her tail curled.

For this doggy was simply too shy.
She did not really understand why
    This was all going on.
    She just wanted to yawn
So she did and then let out a sigh.

The young artist was suddenly rich!
Everyone wanted his bitch!
    But his funds were cut off
    When "The Green Spot" rubbed off
One day when the dog scratched an itch!

Sid then said, "Go on, be free!"
She was happy and all full of glee.
    She knew in her gut
    She was really a mutt
And felt free as the fish in the sea!

So the Wolfaraner went away.
For two years the black dog was a stray.
    She lived on the street,
    And scavenged to eat.
But then something strange happened one day.

As she gnawed a large bone of a roan,
She felt so alone she did moan;
    Then had a great urge—
    An emotional surge—
To let out a loud, resonant tone.

She did and then joined a wolf pack,
For she knew she could never go back
    To living with man;
    They just wanted her tan,
But she knew she'd forever be black.

109
THE TINY YORKIE

There's this tiny, adorable Yorkie
Who lives in Poughkeepsie, New York-y.
    He's now nearly twenty
    (For most dogs that's plenty)
And almost as light as a quark-y.[*]

Well, one day while taking a stroll
He tripped and fell down a deep hole.
    But given his size,
    It was no great surprise
When he landed right next to a mole

Who simply said, "How do you do?"
And the Yorkie said, "Covered with dew."
    So the tiny mole laughed
    So loud that a draft
Was produced and away the dog blew!

The wall he smashed into caved in.
The air in there now seemed quite thin,
    So they dug their way out
    Before they passed out,
And when free, they each had a big grin!

The dog was then asked by the mole
If he could jump through a keyhole.
    So the Yorkie said, "Sure!
    But I'm way too mature
Now to want to do something so droll!"

[*]*Quark: An elementary particle*

61

110
USE YOUR HEAD!

Your puppy's like a two-year-old:
An explorer, inquisitive, bold.
    If she chews up your stuff
    Try not to be rough
And don't punish her, hit her, or scold.

Just buy her some dog toys instead
So she won't go and chew your bedspread.
    If she does, don't yell "No!"
    Say "Off!" and then show
Her a brand new stuffed toy — use your head!

111
THE MALAMUTE

Down the street lives a cute Malamute.
When called she did not give a hoot.
    She did as she pleased.
    Her poor master she teased,
So he said, "I'll just give her a boot!"

He did, and he broke his big toe.
So he called up the dog trainer, Joe.
    The trainer said, "Al,
    Be your dog's pal,
And bring her to me. I'm a pro."

The Malamute's name is Adele.
She learned very quickly and well.
    When Al took her back
    He gave her a snack
And then vowed not to hit, kick, or yell.

But one day he just lost his cool.
He yelled and he screamed like a fool.
    This all hurt his voice,
    And he did not rejoice
'Cause his voice became quite minuscule.

His wonderful, big Malamute
Has since become very astute:
    She watches Al's hand
    As it gives a command,
For her master's now called, "Al the Mute."

112
AT THE PLAYGROUND

At the playground my dog loves the slide
With rolling pins. It's quite a ride!
    He slides on four feet.
    He's quite an athlete
Though he sometimes just jumps off the side.

But last week my big dog had collided
With a kid who was very nearsighted.
    The boy was unhurt
    But he dirtied his shirt.
To that playground we're no more invited.

113
MAN OVERBOARD!

Scott's giant Newfie named Spot
Made him fall out of his yacht.
    While swimming about

He looked up at Spot's snout
And yelled, "Spot, you damn fool, thanks a lot!"

But then Spot from the yacht jumped out, too,
And fell in the ocean so blue
    And pulled Scott to the boat
    While he kept him afloat
And then water from their noses they blew.

Scott then said, "Don't jump on me
'Cause I might just fall into the sea!"
    Then Spot wagged his tail
    And Scott looked at the sail
And said, "Wind's good, so let's have a spree!"

114
PRAISE WORKS

You can teach your new puppy your ways
With treats and a whole lot of praise
    When he does what you like;
    So when your little tyke
Grows up he will truly amaze!

115
HER OWN FAULT

As her Schnauzer was having a scrape
With a Terrier over a crepe
    The woman was bit
    Though she'd later admit
That she shouldn't have grabbed her dog's nape.

116
NO!

My nine-month-old Rottie was naughty;
He ate all of my fresh manicotti.
    I yelled, "No no no no!"
    Then felt like a schmo,
So I cooked up some more for my Scottie!

117
OK

Okay is a good release word.
Most trainers with this have concurred.
    It means, "Do as you please."
    To teach it's a breeze
Though be careful—he may chase a bird!

118
THE MATS IN HER HAIR

Did the thought to you never occur
That the mats in her hair will recur
    Like the rhymes in this poem
    If you don't use a comb
Every day on your dog's long, thick fur?

119
THE PROPER DIET

A girl by the name of Georgina
Every day fed her doggy farina.
    Spirulina she'd add
    (But only a tad)
'Cause the dog liked it more than Purina.

That doggy was certainly picky.
All dog food he thought tasted icky.
    Georgina tried all
    But then gave him to Paul
Who then gave him to someone named Vicki

Who now gives the dog grains and meat
And veggies and garlic to eat.
    The meat he eats raw,
    And big bones he will gnaw,
So now this dog's diet's complete.

120
THAT SURELY MUST HURT!

They howl and growl and whine,
And they grunt and they bark and that's fine;
    They also do yelp
    When they need all your help
After nabbing a large porcupine.

121
A FUNNY HAIRCUT

Poodles sure do love the water!
They swim just as well as an otter.
    They bring in the ducks
    (But not the woodchucks)
Though their haircut could not be much odder.

122
LIKE A CANARY IN A COAL MINE

Though your dog doesn't have a "sixth sense,"
The five he *does* have are intense.
    With an imminent storm
    His mood may transform
From a calm state to one that's quite tense.

He might start to get nervous and pace
With a very big grin on his face
    (Which could indicate fear).
    He may just disappear.
You might not find your dog in your place.

But the point is that dogs have such fine,
Sharp senses that your dog or mine
    Will most likely alert us
    To things that might hurt us.
They're just like that bird in the mine.

123
SHAKE SOMEWHERE ELSE!

The doggy came out of the brook
And ran up to his master and shook.
    The man got all wet
    But was not too upset,
Though he gave that dog one dirty look.

124
THE WEST HIGHLAND WHITE TERRIER

The tough little West Highland White
Can give a big badger a fight!
    Though bred for the farm,
    He has so much charm,
As a pet he will fit in just right.

His heritage sure was pugnacious!
With foxes this dog was tenacious!
    He's so full of vigor
    And such a good digger
He'll burrow to China, good gracious!

He surely will get pretty gritty.
His white fur then will not look so pretty.
    But don't bathe him too often
    'Cause his fur will then soften
And curl, which would be a great pity!

125
LEADER OF THE PACK

If your dog does not think you're the leader
Say, "Sit!" just before you go feed 'er.
    If she doesn't comply
    Then her food just deny
So she'll be more submissive and sweeter.

126
WARM-BLOODED CREATURE

My dog is a warm-blooded creature;
In cold weather, a very good feature.
    But if day turns to night
    And she's still out of sight
And her ears get frostbite — *that* would teach 'er!

127
DOG-TALK

Muscles taut? Tail is held high?
He's staring you right in the eye?
    At his eyes don't stare back
    'Cause he may just attack
And end up with a piece of your thigh!

But if wagging his tail side to side,
And he's "bowing," don't be terrified.
    If his tail is held low
    And it moves to and fro
And he's smiling, then no need to hide.

You must know the signs he's displaying
To tell if he's guarding or playing.
    Watch his ears, mouth, and eyes,
    And what his tail implies,
So you'll know what the doggy is saying.

128

A PUPPY'S TAIL

(If maiming's too gruesome a thought —
If the thought of it makes you distraught —
Then skip over the next
Poem in the text,
But the story's true, like it or not!)

Is docking our tails a good practice?
Or is it just really malpractice?
    Our tails we do need
    So others can read
Whether they should avoid or contact us.

Did you know with our tails we can talk?
So why do you think you should dock
    Our tails? It's insane!
    It causes us pain.
Just the thought of it's even a shock!

Our tail's an important creation.
We use it for communication.
    Our tail can express
    What our mood is unless
It's been docked, which for me's mutilation.

Rome was where docking began
By an agriculturalist man.
    When they bit off its tail

That poor puppy did wail!
But this cruelty they did not yet ban.

The tendons in tails look like worms.
Folks could not with this come to terms;
    So they pulled the "worms" out,
    Which they thought without doubt
Would protect them from rabies—"Bad germs!"

The tendons in tails are all white.
These wormlike things gave folks a fright.
    The man, Columella,
    Was quite an odd fella
'Cause pup's tails he'd have people bite.

A pup would be just four days old
When the "docker" would go grab a hold
    Of the poor puppy's tail.
    If the puppy was frail,
When docked, it might pass right out cold.

Some dock our tails "to prevent
An injury" in the event
    That our tail hits a wall
    Or is grabbed in a brawl,
But these traumas are not that frequent.

Some people think that dewclaws
Should be cut off also just because
    They might just get torn,
    So when we are born
They grab our small paws and don't pause.

Should they also then cut off our toes?
'Cause we might injure those, too—who knows?
    If they cut off our ears
    We will shed some big tears
But some folks do that, too—for shows.

Some folks think shrinking the size
Of our tails may just win them a prize.

God forbid one is kinked!
Or in some way distinct,
Since a club's goal is to standardize.

Some do it for reasons cosmetic
Or for looks that they think are aesthetic;
    But it's just a tradition,
    And then in addition
They don't even use anesthetic.

With tails some folks have a fixation.
They're obsessed with a tail's conformation.
    There's no dog that's flawless
    (Yet most do enthrall us)
But some folks don't want variation.

Since docking is not carved in stone,
Why not our tails leave alone?
    And do not crop our ears
    With those really sharp shears
'Cause we want them intact when we're grown!

129
RUMP-WAG

If in place of a tail there's a stump,
A doggy will then wag his rump.
    His body will wiggle,
    His collar will jiggle;
Excited, he may even jump!

130
SIMBA THE HOUND

When I play my marimba, the sound
Will attract my dog Simba, a hound.
    If I play with good tone
    She'll chew on her bone,
But won't stick around if I pound.

131
POSITIVE TRAINING

You can catch flies much better with honey
Than with vinegar—bet you some money!
    So give him a treat
    Instead of mistreat
The dog that's your friend—okay, sonny?

What I mean is that when he's behaving
Reward him with something he's craving
    Like a ball or a toy,
    Then say "Attaboy!"
But when bad do not go "finger-waving"

Or yelling or squirting or hitting,
'Cause that stuff's not really befitting
    A compassionate handler
    (I'd call it "mis-handler").
Won't work, so you'll feel like just quitting.

132
A QUESTION

What's the difference 'tween a dog and a human?
Does the furry one need extra groomin'?
    Well, the one with four feet
    Seems to need much more meat,
'Cause my mutt stole my steak, and I'm fumin'!

133
A PAIN IN THE BACK

I'm a Dachshund with chronic back pain.
On my delicate spine it's a strain.
    Though my breeder was wrong
    To have made me so long,
Unlike some breeds, I at least have a brain!

134
SHARK

There once was a mongrel named Shark
Who was owned by a fellow named Mark.
    If you gave Shark a treat,
    Your fingers he'd eat
'Cause his bite was much worse than his bark.

135
SAVED BY A TAIL

A dog who ate broccoli and kale
Was arrested and taken to jail —
    Yelled the judge from her seat,
    "You did not eat your meat!" —
But was freed when he wagged his cute tail.

136
WHEN I HAVE BEANS AND RICE, MY DOG GETS DINNER TWICE!

When I feed my dog first, myself last,
My dog eats his dog food up fast;
    And then while I'm eating
    He looks at me, pleading,
And I feel like I'm being harassed!

137
CONNECTING WITH YOUR NEW PUPPY

If you give your new puppy protection,
And teach him and give him affection,
    And protect him from strangers
    And all kinds of dangers,
You'll form a tight bond, a connection.

138
HORSE SENSE

A mongrel was chasing a horse.
The horse was much faster, of course.
    There was some suspense
    As the horse jumped a fence
And escaped, which was par for the course.

The mongrel then stood at the fence
And started to get rather tense.
    That game doggie did bark
    Until it got dark.
His folks knew their mutt rarely relents.

He's now always walked on a lead,
So these folks can control their mixed breed.
    That's just plain horse sense
    So when he smells horse scents
He won't chase those large creatures full speed!

139

MY NEW LITTLE BLACK DEVIL

When last I had been to the shore
A black dog roamed the beach to explore.
    A dolphin hung out
    And frolicked about.
In the sky many sea gulls did soar.

That black dog was a young Schipperkee
Who had turned on his master's TV.
    The show was a bore,
    And his master then swore
He would drown his poor dog in the sea!

So he took that black dog to the ocean
On a boat that was rocking with motion.
   While the boat's engine roared,
   Tossed the dog overboard.
(So much for that monster's devotion!)

After throwing the dog in the drink,
The man quickly took off. What a fink!
   Though he knew how to swim,
   The dog tired of limb,
And of drowning was right on the brink!

But a dolphin quite free and carefree
Just then happened to happen to see,
   And brought the dog back
   To shore on her back.
That black devil's now living with me!

140
BOOMER

A very big mongrel named Boomer
Was forcibly brought to the groomer.
   The dog was so scared
   His canines he bared,
And bit! Or is that just a rumor?

141
A STRONG SWIMMER

There once was a brown Chesapeake
Retriever who swam in a creek.
   Though his master did shout,

He refused to come out,
And he stayed in that creek for a week.

He eventually swam to the bay —
The Chesapeake Bay — to find prey.
    He pursued many geese,
    But the doggy police
Were by now searching every which way.

Completely absorbed in his swim,
Yet in danger, way out on a limb,
    The Chessie had fun
    In the waves and the sun,
But things were about to turn grim.

In a life vest he should have been dressed,
For he suddenly felt he must rest.
    He was miles from shore,
    And so tired and sore,
Just to stay afloat seemed like a test!

With his circumstance more and more dire,
For geese he had no more desire.
    He began to go down.
    If he stopped he would drown,
So kept moving for fear he'd expire.

If he sank where it's deep and it's dark,
He'd be a good snack for a shark —
    A nice, tasty dish
    For a big, hungry fish —
And it wouldn't be scared of his bark!

He was truly in trouble by now,
And hoped he'd be rescued somehow.
    He was barely afloat,
    When along came a boat
With his master, agog, at the bow.

"Look! There's my dog!" the man cried,
Fearing by now he had died.

The big dope was then roped;
He struggled and groped,
And was finally pulled starboard side.

As the dog was pulled onto the boat,
He coughed sea water up from his throat,
Then went home and felt snug
As a bug in a rug
In his dog bed, and that's all she wrote.

142
I'LL TRY NOT TO CRY

My dog is a horrible beast!
'Cause he just had a wonderful feast
On my large pizza pie,
But I'll try not to cry,
For he left me the onions, at least.

143
TICKS

If your doggy is bit by a tick,
Your doggy could get very sick.
The kind that likes deer
Is the kind we all fear.
If you see one, best pick it off quick!

They're spidery, black, and quite small,
And exceedingly slow when they crawl.
On your dog one can climb.
He could end up with Lyme
In the winter, spring, summer, or fall.

Nosodes* may give him protection
So your dog doesn't get an infection.
    They're little white pills
    That prevent many ills,
And much safer than some gross injection.

A homeopathic remedy.

144
DOG DAYS

If in the dog days of summer your pet
Gets no water or shade, I will bet
    When it's ninety degrees
    Without even a breeze,
He will suffer and you'll need the vet.

145
BLAIZE

There once was a doggy named Blaize
Who would sleep in the driveway and laze.
    She would lie on the tar
    Right next to the car
To catch the sun's wonderful rays.

When the landscapers worked on Mondays
Noisy mowers could not that dog faze.
    But, alas, her own master
    Drove over and past 'er,
And that was the end of her days.

146
WHEN HE'S OLD HE MIGHT NOT
HEAR MY CALL

The neighbor's machines make such noise,
I can't even think! It annoys.
    The decibels pound
    On my ear drums with sound,
And my doggy's poor ears it destroys.

Though my dog loves to lie in the sun,
The noisy machines are no fun.
    In the driveway he sleeps
    While the leaf blower keeps
On blowing the dust till they're done.

When he's old he might not hear my call,
Or the bounce of his old tennis ball.
    'Cause he lives in a place
    Where noise slaps one's face
Like running smack into a wall!

147
A MUDDY MUTT

When she saw her dog rolling in muck
The woman was quite horror-struck.
    The dog was so muddy
    That his human buddy
Just uttered one syllable: "Yuck!"

148
IT'S THE MAN WHO IS BAD

Pit Bulls are nice until taught
To be mean by thugs who should be caught.
    So no need to ban
    The breed. It's the man
Who's bad, not the cute puppy he bought.

149
UNACCEPTABLE BEHAVIOR

Objects for me imperceptible
At night, for my dog are perceptible.
    When he dashes away
    In the dark after prey,
And he won't come back — that's unacceptable!

150
JUMPING

Kneeing your dog in the chest
Would not be considered the best
    Approach. It's not cool.
    In fact it's quite cruel.
There's a better way trainers suggest:

Instead of all jumps being banned
Teach him to jump on command.
    Say the word, "Up!"
    So your fast-growing pup
Jumps when *you* want. Would that not be grand?

Unless you say, "Up!" to implore him,
If he jumps on you simply ignore him.
    It's really preferred
    That you not say a word,
But if your dog sits, then adore him!

151
AN IMAGINARY POLICE OFFICER'S POETIC MUSINGS ON POLICE DOGS AND THE GOOD WORK OF THEIR FRIEND, STEPHANIE TAYLOR

A police dog should wear a good vest,
Or he might get a wound in his chest.
    Though off-duty he's frisky,
    His job is quite risky.
Bullet and stab-proof is best.

A ten-year-old girl, Stephanie,
Has raised thousands of dollars, you see,
    So our dogs can have vests.
    She gets many requests
From the dogs' human partners like me.

Stephanie's very relieved
To know hundreds of dogs have received
    Some defense from gunfire,
    So their lives won't expire.
It's amazing what she has achieved!

152
I JUST CAN'T WATCH

While my dog gets superb exercise
When he's hunting, I just agonize,
 'Cause I can't stand the thought
 Of the thing being caught,
So I just don't watch—I close my eyes.

153
SPOT'S ANTICS

My friend gave my pup something hot:
Some scalding soup, right from the pot.
 The pup burnt his tongue,
 Which then sort of just hung,
And the look he gave said, "Thanks a lot!"

Said my friend, "Your dog learned a good rule."
I said, "Yeah, don't take things from a fool?"
 "OK, I was wrong,"
 Said my friend before long.
"From now on I shall wait till it's cool."

But the pup came right back to drink more,
Though I'm sure his tongue still felt quite sore.
 Though he needed some leverage
 To get to the beverage,
He did manage three licks or four.

The next day the pup came with a trot,
And had more soup, believe it or not.
 And then the young chap
 Went and took a long nap.
Well, I guess that stuff sure hit the spot!

154
THE CONTRACT

If you work for me pulling my sleigh
I'll provide you with shelter and pay
    You with food and take care
    Of you. Is that not fair?
And I'll be your friend. What do you say?

Great! Now start pulling my sled!
OK, now pull, go ahead.
    Hurry up, MUSH!
    I'm in a big rush!
Quit acting like you're made of lead!

Why aren't you moving, you mutt?
Do you want a good kick in the butt?
    Ah, no wonder we're not
    Moving, we got
Stuck in a very deep rut.

So even though we didn't get
To go even two inches yet,
    I'll give you a treat
    'Cause you seem kind of beat.
Will we get there perhaps by sunset?

All right, we will just go and walk.
On the way we will have a good talk.
    I'll go and unstrap you,
    Or should I just slap you?
No matter, my car's down the block.

155
LADY

There once was a Shepherd named Lady
Who had saved a young lady named Sadie
    From a man with a knife
    Who tried taking her life,
One dark night, long ago, in New Haiti.

Young Sadie was taking a stroll
For exercise — that was her goal.
    She breathed in the cool air,
    The breeze ruffled her hair,
But a cop should have been on patrol!

For on reaching the very next street,
A man pushed her right off of her feet.
    He then grabbed her throat
    While he took from his coat
A very big knife made for meat.

The girl had no clue what to do.
She was certain her life was now through!
    The man, who was large,
    Felt completely in charge,
When a dog charged from out of the blue!

That evening seemed blacker than coal.
There was no one in sight, not a soul.
    Sadie started to scream.
    This all seemed like a dream.
But the Shepherd was now in control!

She jumped on the man with such force,
He thought he'd been struck by a horse!
    The dog's teeth were now bared,
    And the man was so scared,
He attempted his only recourse:

He got up and tried running away.
But the Shepherd pursued him like prey.
    The dog was now chasing
    The man who was racing
Towards docks at the edge of the bay.

Though the man tried to stop at the dock,
He plunged into the bay like a rock!
    The dog then returned
    To the girl who had learned
It's not safe to walk even one block!

The stray had some small wounds to mend,
And Sadie thought, *She needs a friend.*
    When she took the dog in,
    The dog licked her chin,
And together, twelve years they did spend!

Said Sadie, who's now in her eighties,
Having tea with the ladies at Katie's,
    "If that dog didn't scare
    That mean mugger, I swear
I would not be here now with you ladies!"

156
DINING IN CHINA

They are serving me "chow" meat in China.
I think it will give me angina!
    Where is my dog now?
    I can't find my Chow Chow!
I sure hope he's in North Carolina!

That's where we lived by the way
Till we moved on the first day of May
    To China by ship;

Though a nice enough trip,
My brown hair is now turning all gray,

'Cause my Chow Chow was right by my foot,
But he disappeared, didn't stay put.
    He is no where around.
    The dog cannot be found.
Is the bond between us now kaput?

It was not all that strong anyway.
My Chow Chow would just never stay
    Too long by my side.
    He would roam far and wide,
And be gone for twelve hours a day.

I just got a call from a friend;
My doggie's days did not yet end.
    He'd snuck onto a cruiser
    And slept—he's a snoozer.
On crew members he did depend

For water and all kinds of food,
And he even got bones that he chewed.
    He's now back in the town
    Where he'd once roamed aroun'
And I'm now in a much better mood!

157
GINNY, THE CAT-SAVING HERO

A Terrier-Husky called Ginny
Rescues poor homeless cats, mostly skinny,
    Abandoned and scared,
    Abused or impaired.
This doggy already saved many.

The cats that this doggy will pick
Are the ones that are crippled or sick.

She will groom the poor things,
Which much joy to them brings;
From nose to tail those cats she'll lick.

Trapped under glass that was shattered,
At the bottom of a box that was tattered,
Was a kitten, alive!
How did she survive?
Ginny pawed her way down, her paws spattered.

Ginny is so dedicated
To rescuing cats isolated,
She'll risk her own skin
For those felines like kin.
That cat-savior's quite celebrated.

Note: You can read all about Ginny in The Dog Who Rescues Cats *by Philip Gonzalez and Leonore Fliescher (New York: HarperCollins, 1995).*

158
THE DALSATIAN

There once was a dog from Alsatia
In love with a dog from Dalmatia.
They were such an odd pair
You could not help but stare,
And the shy couple moved to Croatia.

But they fared even worse over there,
Although now they did not seem to care.
Though people would jeer
And throw bottles of beer,
The two dogs were not even aware,

Until one of them finally got hit.
Startled, the dog turned and bit.
So they moved once again,

Dug a large den,
And gave birth to eight puppies, quite fit.

They took excellent care of their tots
Which looked like white Shepherds with spots.
    They'd go out every day,
    Hunting for prey,
And the puppies ate well—there was lots.

Though intelligent, agile, and spry,
These dogs were, by nature, quite shy,
    Which perhaps was OK,
    'Cause a hunter might slay
One or more of them—they could all die!

But the fears that they had were allayed
Just as soon as they frolicked and played,
    Which they did quite a bit.
    When exhausted they'd quit,
And then snooze in their den or some shade.

But some days were not all that easy.
When hunters lurked, it made them queasy.
    Though they rarely were seen
    By those jerks who were mean,
Their presence still made them uneasy.

Though their life's become hard, they're content—
They're surviving in any event.
    Dalsatians, quite wild,
    If approached become riled,
For they don't, of course, trust your intent.

A Dalsatian's life span is not long,
And hunting them surely is wrong;
    They're social and smart,
    And they almost make art—
When they howl, it's like a great song!

The Dalsatian is such a rare breed,
You won't find him in books you might read.

They live on the prairie,
Are shy and quite wary,
So haven't yet been pedigreed.

159
ON TOP OF THE ROOF

My corpulent mutt who's aloof
Is now sitting on top of the roof.
    How did he get there?
    Did he fly through the air?
Was it some kind of magic — a spoof?

The large beast in our attic, unseen,
Tore through a small window screen.
    Perhaps I will just
    Leave him there till he must
Have some food and he's finally lean!

160
NO SHOCK TREATMENT PLEASE!

"Shock me again and I'll bite!"
And that doggy would really be right.
    There's a more humane way
    To get dogs to obey:
It's called positive training. All right?

If you shock your dog often, you jerk,
He'll go crazy, go nuts, go berserk.
    Use a "clicker" and treat
    Your good dog to some meat.
It takes patience, it's fun, it's teamwork.

You and your dog are a team.
When he does well, then praise him — he'll beam!
    Break it down into steps
    Until he accepts
You as teacher, and please do not scream!

161
NOT ONE TO MESS WITH

I know a large Shepherd named Zak
Who will bark at you, yet won't attack
    Unless there's a cue
    From his master named Drew,
And then pray that big dog is called back!

But if Zak were to misread a cue
From Drew, he just might attack you!
    If Drew's not alert
    You or I could get hurt,
And then someone would probably sue.

Zak's teeth are quite large, his jaws strong.
To his owner do not do a wrong,
    Unless you like dying,
    Or in the ground, lying.
If smart, you'll just move right along.

To Drew's friends Zak is friendly and sweet.
He'll give them his paw for a treat;
    But break into Drew's pad,
    Well, friend, that would be sad,
'Cause your meat is what Big Zak would eat!

Barking is quite adequate
To deter any burglar — he'd quit
    His attempt to break in —

He'd not even begin!
If he heard a dog barking, he'd split!

But Zak is a danger to all,
For he doesn't just bark, he will maul.
    By mistake he might charge
    The wrong person, like Marge,
Drew's neighbor who lives down the hall.

Were Zak to attack unprovoked,
With a "death-needle" he would be poked.
    Were Zak to be taken
    Drew's heart would be breakin' —
His face, from big tears, would be soaked.

But don't mess with that dog, OK, friend?
Or your life may just suddenly end.
    They call him Big Zak,
    He is trained to attack,
And don't ever his master offend!

162
AGILITY

Can your doggy develop ability
To master a course in agility?
    If she has speed and control,
    Lots of spirit and soul,
Then your dog will, in all probability.

163
CAPE HUNTING DOGS

Conspicuously mottled they are,
So they're easily seen from afar.
    The Cape hunting dogs
    Hang out by the bogs.
They're black, brown, and white — how bizarre!

Their spotting makes quite a hodgepodge
Of colors resembling collage.
    Each dog is unique,
    They look awfully chic —
Quite conspicuous — no camouflage!

An artist like Vincent van Gogh
Could have made a great painting, you know,
    Of a large pack of fifty,
    Their patterns so nifty,
The sun almost sets them aglow!

Maybe a painter like Pollock
Could have captured these dogs when they frolic,
    Which, when done all their life,
    Keeps them free of much strife
In a land that is fairly bucolic.

If you watch them, you'll readily see
That family life is the key
    To getting along,
    For they know they belong
To the pack which, on grasslands, roams free.

The den that they make's recreated
From burrows extant but vacated
    By some other life form
    And now is kept warm
By the Cape hunting dogs who have mated.

They give birth to a very large litter,
And then feed and take care of each critter.
    I refer to the young
    Who are cleaned with the tongue
Of their mother or her puppy-sitter.

The puppies get lots of attention
From adults in the pack, not to mention
    Being fed every day
    With the meat from the prey
The adults chase and hunt by convention.

When the grown-ups come back with the meat
They scramble and stumble, compete
    To play with and feed
    The puppies — indeed
They'll trip over each other's big feet!

When playing, they twitter and squeak,
And chatter like birds in a clique.
    When lost they go, "Hoo,
    I'm here. Where are you?"
And they bark, which means "Hark!" so to speak.

They hunt for their food by their wit,
For a zebra that's young or unfit.
    Up to two days they'll trot
    On savannas, quite hot,
After prey — these strong dogs rarely quit.

To prepare for a hunt they will nuzzle
And lick one another's broad muzzle.
    They get very excited
    When zebras are sighted.
(To me that's not much of a puzzle.)

While moving around a large herd
The Cape hunting dogs, self-assured,
    Will stealthily slink
    So slow they don't blink,
While observing their prey (take my word).

When they spot a large beast that looks "right"
They'll sprint towards that zebra and bite.
    Disemboweling's their plan;
    They'll bite off what they can.
With tails wagging, the poor beast they'll smite.

They'll bring back lots of meat which they'll share
With the young and the old—that's just fair,
    Then frolic and play
    For the rest of the day.
As for zebras tomorrow? BEWARE!

164
IS HER COAT MADE OF DOG FUR?

Don't you know that fur coat on your wife
Was an animal, vital, a life?
    That coat made of fur
    Might have been a dog, sir,
And, sadly, the fur trade's still rife.

Two million dogs and cats killed
In the world every year, their blood spilled,
    For their fur's a disgrace
    To our great human race
(Though Cruella De Vil would be thrilled).

But congress has passed a provision
To ban dog and cat fur—good decision.
    Perhaps we'll soon see
    All animals free
From bloodshed—a wonderful vision!

If your wife would her fur coat donate
To a soul who's misfortune or fate
    Made her homeless and cold,
    Or sick or just old,
Some suffering might, therefore, abate.

165
NIGHT VISION

In the dark, my dog's eyes sometimes shine —
Much more than your eyes do or mine.
    A reflecting device
    Lets him see cats or mice
Or raccoons on which he'd love to dine!

So my dog sees quite well in the dark,
Like at dusk when we walk through the park.
    (He also hears things —
    Perhaps a bat's wings —
And he'll stop and sniff every dog's mark.)

While in daylight he barely sees tints
Of faint colors, pastel, when he squints,
    At night he'll detect
    Some fleeting object,
And then suddenly takes off and sprints.

But the creature he's after will freeze,
While it's thinking, *Don't kill me now please!*
    It's so still, he can't see it —
    If he could, he would tree it.
And the creature thinks, *Hope I don't sneeze!*

But if it tries fleeing, however,
My dog would then make an endeavor —
    While its movement he sees
    In the grass or the trees —
To pursue the poor creature forever!

Though I know my dog soon will return,
I still try my best to discern
    Where he'd likely now be,
    Yet I can't even see
Past the edge of the path and some fern.

But my dog has no problem at night,
Whether midnight or dawn or twilight.
    His eyes are so keen
    They take in the whole scene.
While I can't see a thing, he sees LIGHT!

166
A TIRED DOG'S A QUIET DOG

Down the street lives a Sheltie named Parker
Who's owner's been trying to spark 'er
    Interest in toys,
    'Cause the doggy annoys
The whole neighborhood — she's such a barker!

But for other than doing her "stuff,"
The poor dog doesn't get out enough.
    Though she's really adored,
    She's also quite bored,
And she's putting on weight from foodstuff.

But her misguided owner named Chet
Doesn't yet get that his pet
    Needs to run and to play
    Three hours a day —
For a tired dog's quiet, I'll bet.

167
FLYBALL

All kinds of dogs learn flyball.
They must know how to do a recall.
    "It sure is great fun
    To catch balls and to run!"
And be friendly — we don't want a brawl!

168
CITY GOES TO THE DOGS

In Romania's capital city
There's a sight that is truly a pity:
    Stray dogs roaming free
    By the thousands, you see,
So keep a close eye on your kitty!

People have gotten attacked
By the dogs, this is true, it's a fact.
    There are more and more strays
    On the streets nowadays,
So Mayor Basescu will act.

Romanians, known for their love
Of animals, won't get rid of
    The dogs in the street
    That scavenge for meat,
But a plan has been made by their gov.

A sterilization program
(Though it may cause some doggies to scram)
    Will be soon implemented,
    So mating prevented,
And dogs will keep roaming — hot damn!

But catching the dog's won't be easy,
And the caught dogs will feel quite uneasy;
    'Cause a mere twenty men
    Will catch one now and then,
And the dogs, tranquilized, may feel queasy;

But thank God not one dog will be killed!
The people and dogs will be thrilled.
    Those folks have a heart,
    The dogs are street smart,
And the mayor's goal will be fulfilled.

169
WHAT A NOSE!

I'm glad his butt's covered with hair
'Cause it's sticking way up in the air.
    He's digging a hole,
    But what is his goal?
Is it food? If it is, he won't share;

'Cause he pulled out a filthy brown thing
Which he shook so the dirt doesn't cling;
    Then ran off to hide
    With that piece of rawhide.
When I find him, his neck I will wring!

170
A DOG THAT LIKES VARIETY

My intelligent Rhodesian Ridge
Can open the door of the fridge.
    I actually saw
    Him using his paw
To pry the door open a smidge.

He then, with his nose, made the door
Open further so he could explore
    The wonderful scents
    Of the fridge's contents,
And made milk spill all over the floor,

Which he lapped up as fast as he could.
Last Friday he drank all the Hood,
    The Sealtest on Sunday,
    The Garelick Monday —
And yet he's not sick! Knock on wood!

171
NO WAY IMPROVED

While domestic dogs live in our homes,
The genes in our pet's chromosomes
    Are not that removed,
    And in no way improved,
From the wolf that in north country roams.

172
THE DREAM

My dog, sound asleep, softly snoring,
While outside the cold rain keeps on pouring,
    Is on his dog bed,
    Which is blue with some red.
Perhaps in his dream he is soaring.

While floating way high in midair,
With the wind blowing through his long hair,
    He's looking aroun'
    Though mostly straight down,
And asks, "How many species are there

"Of canids all over the earth
Which humans consider of worth?
    From the wolf came the breeds
    Which man made for his needs
By selecting which dogs would give birth.

"Of breeds there is quite a selection,
And most of us dogs get affection
    From our surrogate pack
    Who will give us a snack
If we're good, but if bad, a correction.

"I can see all of Earth's goings on,
From Iran to the hot Amazon;
    And I will predict
    (Though the thought gets me ticked)
That Earth's creatures will one day be gone.

"So who will share man's lonely days?
Why, us dogs of course (even the strays)."
    My dog then awoke,
    And I gave him a stroke
Down his neck, though he seemed in a daze.

But then suddenly my dear old pet
Licked my face, and I'll make you a bet
    That he wants to go out,
    And I haven't a doubt
That outside he'll get pretty darn wet!

173
A MUSICIAN

Wolves are quite knit by tradition.
(Of humans they have much suspicion.)
    They're social like us,
    And intelligent; thus
When one howls, he's like a musician.

174
THE RESEARCH LAB

Pesticides they want to test
On my friend who I'd often caressed.
    They took him away
    When he went out to play,
And I'm very upset and depressed.

From right under my nose he was taken,
And my heart is now painfully breakin'.
    Some jerk in a cab
    Sold my dog to a lab—
A place of torture, Godforsaken.

My dog is so friendly and trusting,
His tail he would wag while they're thrusting
    Into him some injection
    To prime him for dissection.
These scum bags sure do things disgusting

To innocent creatures they nab,
Like my wonderful dog, a black Lab.
    Where is he now?
    I must free him somehow.
I will go there and then my dog grab.

The research lab's just down the street.
I'll notify PETA, we'll meet.
    We'll break down their big door,
    Grab my big Labrador,
And make a run for it, retreat.

Would they shoot us, or chase us, or what?
I don't know, but we'll take a short cut
    Back to my place.
    Though it might be a race,
We'll run in, and my door I will shut.

The next day our large group did just that.
For us it was nothing, old hat!
    'Cause we're P-E-T-A.
    We're tough, we don't play!
And cruelty we'll always combat.

My dog is now safely inside
My house where, for now, he will hide.
    The police will soon nab
    Those jerks from the lab,
And to jail they're soon going to ride.

175
A WOLF IN DISGUISE

Your dog is a wolf in disguise!
Why is that such a surprise?
    Because they're one species,
    If watching, you'll see she's
A tame wolf with big friendly eyes!

176
A CONSULTATION WITH THE DOG
BEHAVIORIST

"If I was a millionaire,
When she chews up my things I'd not care,
    But the fact that I'm not
    Means I'll just have to swat
Her with rolled-up newspapers, I swear!

"When my dog gets a hold of my stuff
I just cannot help but be rough.
    I'm just not that rich

So when my little bitch
Destroys things, I give her a cuff.

"The dog's only bad when I'm out."
When your shopping or working, no doubt.
    "Yes, and when I come back
    I give her a whack,
'Cause I find a huge mess and I shout ..."

But, my friend, that's plain cruel, ineffective!
Look at it from her perspective:
    Your dog has no clue
    Why your top you just blew,
So that's just not a useful corrective.

Yelling and hitting won't work,
And they're very abusive, you jerk!
    So I would refrain
    From causing her pain,
For your doggy might just go berserk.

Plus, if you don't catch your dog in the act —
If you wait until after the fact —
    Then she simply won't know
    Why you carry on so,
And when teaching her try to have tact.

You could tell her it's just not acceptable
To chew all your things, though delectable.
    Better yet, hide
    Those things she's denied
So it's out of her sight — undetectable.

It's possible your dog is prone
To anxiety when left alone.
    When you leave, be low-key
    And she'll be worry-free
And contentedly chew on her bone.

But if she keeps on raiding your trash,
Before you blow up or act rash,

Consider the cause
Of her actions, and pause,
Take a breath, and do not at her lash.

Like a wolf cub, your dog was exploring,
For otherwise her days are boring.
    She needs more activity.
    From much inactivity
Your dog excess fat will start storing.

Why don't you tire her out
With walks? Every day a new route.
    Twice a day would be great,
    Get her nose working, mate.
With her nose she'll explore all about.

By the time she gets home, she'll be tired,
And you yourself will be perspired.
    So for hours she'll snooze
    As though she had booze.
Is that not what you wanted, desired?

When you're gone keep your dog occupied
By searching for treats that you hide.
    She'll have lots of fun,
    And when finally done
With her search, she'll be quite pacified.

When going to work, or whatever,
Be creative and do something clever:
    Give your dog a neat toy
    Like a Buster Cube. Boy!
It would change her behavior forever!

When you finally come home again,
She'll look forward to seeing you then.
    And you won't get all mad
    And so make her feel bad,
And your bond will be stronger, amen!

That'll be eighty bucks, sir.
Though I take checks, it's cash I prefer.
    Well, I wish your dog well.
    I'm sure she'll do swell!
But call if your problems recur.

177
KOOL

There once was a Poodle named Kool
Who if tempted with cookies would drool.
    If you were to renege
    On his treat while he'd beg,
On the floor you'd see quite a large pool.

178
CANIS LUPUS: THE ORIGINAL DOG

In a great northern forest of pine
Live magnificent creatures, lupine.
    They're not easily seen
    In their homeland, pristine,
Whether twilight or dusk or sunshine.

In the Ice Age the wolf was our friend.
In the hunt his great skill he would lend.
    Wolves ran so darn fast
    They would man flabbergast—
In the hunt they sure held up their end!

The Pleistocene hunters, fur-clad,
Heard some tunes which were not all that bad
    From wolves that were stringing

Along and were "singing,"
Which frequently formed a triad.

When, with spears, human hunters took aim
And killed a large mammoth, their game,
    The wolves would collect
    All the meat they'd reject,
And would eat it without any shame.

For wolves, herding prey is a breeze.
Men watched them do it with ease.
    Men would then spear
    The prey that was near,
And say, "Do it again, would you please?"

So the best herding wolves were selected.
Their herding instinct was perfected
    To such a degree
    It is not hard to see
That wolves were, by hunters, respected.

(Later, when people had sheep,
Their dogs would defend, they would keep
    The flocks safe and sound,
    So men kept them around,
And with peace of mind shepherds could sleep.)

The number of wolves was the same
As the men who killed off the big game.
    But people then sought
    The same prey the wolves brought
To their cubs (which some folks tried to tame).

Humans now had a big fear
That the wolves would eat all of the deer
    So that man would have none,
    Unless with his gun
He could shoot all the wolves that were near.

Suddenly there was a war
Between man and the wolves in our lore;

For man now encroached
On wolves' land — even poached
Them — and the friendship we had was no more.

When the north people started invading,
Wolves might have been congregating
    And watching those men
    And women back then.
In ambush they may have been waiting.

A lone person would not have a prayer
Against a wolf pack which could tear
    That man limb from limb,
    But if they should spare him,
He might tell other folks to beware

Of dangerous man-eating creatures
With large jaws and sharp teeth their main features.
    The bold wolves were then slain,
    Only shy ones remain,
So the cruel acts of man were wolves' teachers.

Thus, the number of wolves is now small,
Though in places you'll still hear their call.
    Yet some jerks, for a thrill,
    Even now want to kill
Those magnificent dogs, one and all.

But some people really do yearn
For a time when the wolves will return,
    But if wolves disappear
    And no more reappear,
Perhaps a big lesson we'll learn.

About wolves are great stories, mythology,
And they're closely observed in ethology;
    But will they survive?
    Or will they all dive
Towards the grave and not hear our apology?

179
THERE AREN'T MANY LEFT

Although wolves are by nature gregarious,
Men make their lives quite precarious.
    There aren't many left,
    Of land they're bereft,
And the ways people kill them are various.

180
RUN FOR YOUR LIFE

Universal is wolf's fear of man,
Whether hunter or your neighbor, Stan.
    A wolf has but one
    Defense, which is run
From a group of mean men—futile plan!

181
THERE WON'T BE ONE

Genocide's what man has done
To the wolf with his spear and his gun.
    Though there are still a few
    Here and there, it is true,
If we don't act soon, there won't be one!

If wolves go extinct we'll soon follow.
If that omen is too hard to swallow,
    Then think about this:
    If our chance we all miss
To save them, our lives would be hollow.

182
CRY "WOLF!"

"Wolf!" is what that bad boy cries
'Cause the image of wolf terrifies;
    But why is it scary?
    He's no adversary!
Though "sportsmen" shoot him for a prize.

Is "Wolf!" what our scientists cry
When they tell us the earth will soon die?
    When those folks predict doom
    Should we all just assume
They are right and give up—say "Good-bye?"

But, alas, "Wolf!" is not what they're crying,
For our planet is actually dying!
    By the wayside wolves fall
    With earth's animals—ALL!
And the thought of it's too horrifying!

If humans survive the ordeal
How would those people then feel?
    They'd likely be lonely,
    For they'd be the only
Life form on this planet, for real!

But that is not totally true,
For there would be someone else, too.
    The dog, man's best friend,
    Would stay to the end,
Unless there were no bones to chew.

183
A TIME OUT

If your dog is unruly don't shout.
Instead give your dog a "time out."
    For teachers in school
    "Time out" is a tool
To make the brat calmer, no doubt.

184
LIPS

There once was a Collie named Lips
Who instead of wet kisses gave nips.
    She was pretty darn shy,
    Though no one knew why,
And she didn't have many friendships.

But because of a very kind trainer
Who's goal was to finally gain 'er
    Trust in mankind,
    She felt more inclined
To lick you and acted much saner.

185
A BUFFET

If you don't put your garbage away,
When you're out of the house she will play.
    If her day was quite boring
    She might start exploring
The trash bag and have a buffet.

186

AN ENTHUSIASTIC
PETIT BASSET GRIFFON VENDÉEN

To Michael and Monica Fay, and their dog, Marley

A P.B.G.V. with some brawn,
Marley loves hunting at dawn.
    With her keen big black nose,
    After rabbits she goes,
And before you can blink she is gone!

Though she's small, Marley's speed is quite great.
The gallop's her primary gait.
    When she's after a hare,
    For that hare say a prayer—
Unless Marley already ate.

187

RAGS

Down the street lives a mongrel named Rags
Who now wears some fancy dog tags.
    Though she's very well known,
    Her master, named Sloan,
Used to carry some very large bags.

The bags contained empty tin cans
Of soda or beer, different brands,
    Which he'd bring to a store
    And from the cash drawer
A few dollars and cents would change hands.

With the money he earned he would buy,
For himself and his dog, loaves of rye.
    He would break one in half

And let out a laugh,
And the man and his dog would both sigh.

While Rags ate her half really fast,
Sloan made his half really last.
    Though it took him an hour
    And almost went sour,
He sure did enjoy his repast.

When Rags was a nine-month-old pup,
To a tree her mean folks tied her up.
    Then those jerks moved away,
    And left her to stay
In the yard. The thought's horrible. Yup.

After moving to I-don't-know-where,
It was clear they did not really care
    What happened to her;
    The lonely, young cur
For days had been languishing there ...

But then Sloan, who was homeless and poor,
Found the dog and did love her, for sure!
    The dog loved him, too,
    'Cause the puppy just knew
That this man had a heart that was pure.

When day turned to night and got dark,
The two of them slept in a park.
    The man had few fears,
    For the dog had keen ears;
If a stranger approached she would bark.

Rags had developed great skill
At hunting small prey and would kill
    Things like squirrels or rats
    Or sometimes muskrats,
So her stomach, with meat, she would fill.

When Rags would present things to Sloan,
Like dead mice, he'd just stand there and groan.

He had no taste for mice.
He'd much rather eat rice,
But since he had none, he would moan.

Though attempting to be self-sufficient,
For the most part he had insufficient
    Sources of food
    Which did not help his mood,
And his protein intake was deficient.

For years they had lived in this way,
And Sloan would quite frequently pray
    For himself and his mutt
    To get out of their rut,
For they'd often go hungry all day.

Then one day a famous film maker,
To the poor man said, "I want to take 'er.
    I will make you quite rich
    If you lend me your bitch
'Cause a famous film star I will make 'er."

A movie career did attract 'er
Interest, so she went and packed 'er
    Suitcase and went,
    With her master's consent,
To train and become a great actor.

She won an award, a big prize.
To stardom that mongrel did rise.
    Her career has gone far.
    She became a big star.
About Rags many dogs fantasize.

From ragged to riches they went.
The man's now a dignified gent.
    Instead of rye bread,
    Healthy dog food she's fed,
And they both are now very content.

188
TO CANINES BE KIND

Perhaps the word *dog* in reverse
Is *God* 'cause it's just a perverse
    Coincidence to
    Provide me and you
With this God-awful doggerel verse.

Or perhaps these two words in our mind
Are but one, for it's thought that mankind
    Would have failed, disappeared,
    If dogs hadn't appeared
On the scene — so to canines be kind!

189
BORA

I know a Dalmatian named Bora
Who knocked over his master's menorah.
    The master, dirt poor,
    Just could not this endure,
And then made the poor dog read the Torah.

Bora, while not too religious,
With Hebrew got very prodigious.
    But during a service
    The dog became nervous
And barked, which was quite sacrilegious!

He could no more attend synagogue.
The rabbi said, "Beware of dog!"
    The poor master, dismayed,
    For his doggy then prayed,
And so now they live high on the hog!

190
WHY DOGS DON'T JUST GNAW US

Although man didn't consciously plan it,
Dogs live all over our planet:
    As pets in our home,
    Or as stray dogs that roam,
And coyotes on mountains of granite.

Wherever we go our dog goes,
And our population also grows;
    We in the billions,
    Our dogs in the millions.
Where it will end, no one knows.

From North Pole to South Pole they're found,
Whether Labrador, Husky, or hound,
    Or the feral dingoes,
    Or the purebreds for shows,
Or the ones that end up in the pound.

If an extraterrestrial saw us
They might wonder why dogs don't just gnaw us,
    For canines are stronger
    (Though humans live longer),
Yet dogs for attention just paw us.

'Cause for thousands of years a connection
Grew 'tween humans and dogs to perfection.
    Symbiosis is what
    You have with your mutt,
For you both give each other affection.

191
BUG

I know a small Shih Tzu named Bug
Who always loves getting a hug.
    But he's kind of possessive
    And sometimes aggressive,
And had a big fight with a Pug.

The Pug came by wanting attention
From Bug's owner, which caused apprehension
    In the feisty Shih Tzu
    Whose top simply blew.
So Bug, now, is doing detention.

192
HAVE A LAMB FOR A SNACK

If a sheep dog is not very biddable
He might bite a sheep, not permittable.
    From his master he'll learn
    That from sheep he must turn
Away, though they sure are quite gettable!

Since a flock is a guarding dog's "pack,"
An intruder he'll surely attack;
    But a dog that's a herder
    Would love to just murder
Those sheep—have a lamb for a snack.

193
FROM DUO TO TRIO

I know of a doggy named Drummer
Whose master plays banjo, a strummer.
    The man and his pet
    Were a famous duet.
They toured all around during summer.

The venues they played at were various,
Their performances often hilarious.
    They told lots of jokes
    For appreciative folks,
And were both very friendly, gregarious.

The dog could not only keep time,
At the same time he'd say a neat rhyme.
    The duo was so
    Versatile. Oh!
They even performed pantomime!

But one day there was a big fire
In a place they performed — it was dire.
    The place was aflame,
    And everyone's aim
Was to get out before they expire.

All of the folks got away
Except a small child named Kay.
    When the firemen came
    They called out her name,
And her parents then started to pray.

But the musical dog dashed right in
To the big burning building, an inn.
    The dog found the kid
    Who was buried amid
A bunch of loose rubble therein.

The firemen then pulled her out.
That dog saved her life without doubt.
    Though the girl went through hell,
    The youngster got well.
That dog sure did stick his neck out!

Drummer was certainly brave
To run into the fire to save
    A little girl's life.
    (That girl played the fife,
And folks, for that trio, now rave.)

194
ROCK

Down the street lives a Rottie named Rock
Who listens to Mozart and Bach.
    When he hears minuets
    He will do pirouettes
And then feels like he'd done a spacewalk.

In a fugue when he hears imitation
Rock has a strong inclination,
    Until the fugue's end,
    To play with his friend,
Who happens to be a Dalmatian.

When he hears a piano sonata
Or a symphony or a cantata
    He perks up his ears —
    He'd done it for years —
And he loves to hear songs like "Granada."

When hearing the works of Scarlatti
This sensitive, musical Rottie
    Will wag his short tail

And invite an Airedale
To join him along with a Scottie.

In front of the speakers they lie.
And turn on his master's hi-fi.
       They listen with awe
       While some bones they all gnaw,
And they get quite a musical high.

But once after playing quite hard,
They came into the house from the yard.
       The doggies, quite beat,
       For lunch had some meat,
And then put on some Cage, avant-garde.

Said Rock's master, "I hear no triad.
I think that this music is bad.
       Please turn that stuff off,"
       He said with a scoff,
And the poor guy then went kind of mad.

So the Rottie now lives all alone.
All day he just chews on a bone
       While with very keen ears
       Great music he hears
From his poor master's old gramophone.

All of Rock's friends still drop in.
When he sees them he has a big grin.
       They hang out in the den
       And hear at least ten
LP records per day Rock will spin.

195
ALONG THE LONG PATH
(NEAR TROUT BROOK)

Along the long path in the sun,
Spot and I walked, having fun,
    When a deer Spot did spot.
    Though the weather was hot,
In hot pursuit Spot then did run!

I felt fear; we were near a large street.
And because Spot is ever so fleet,
    I screamed his name ten
    Or more times just then
Mixed with swear words, and not too discreet!

Within minutes my doggy was back.
When I praised him, my hoarse voice did crack!
    The deer was long gone,
    I put his leash on,
And we headed once more down the track.

In the brook Spot did spot a muskrat —
Brown fur, long black tail, and quite fat.
    Against my own will,
    Spot flew down the hill
Dragging me right behind — what a brat!

I tripped and was dragged on the dirt.
"Stop, you durn mutt!" I did blurt.
    But Spot kept on going.
    My anger was growing,
'Cause mud was all over my shirt.

Yet I would not let go of Spot's tether,
Which was made of good quality leather.
    When he finally stopped

I was totally sopped,
But we still, nonetheless, were together!

Spot was having a rather nice day.
He sure tried to get his own way!
    But because of his lead,
    Spot didn't succeed
In catching that muskrat—his prey.

For Spot it was really all play.
Yet I wish he would better obey.
    Though Spot makes me mad,
    He's not really bad—
Just pretends not to hear what I say!

196
GORDON'S JOURNEY

It was raining quite hard as a Setter
Named Gordon got wetter and wetter.
    Later that day
    As the storm moved away
He began to feel better and better.

And yet Gordon thought: *This is not fair!*
'Cause my ears and back legs have long hair.
    Ten giraffes might fly by
    Before I'll get dry!
But my master does not seem to care.

Where is that mean guy anyway?
Is he planning to come home today?
    But in truth, the poor bloke
    Was abducted, no joke,
From a theater while watching a play.

The abductors had travelled quite far,
For these beings had come from a star

Twelve light years away
Called Komondor A,
And they sure didn't come in a car!

In a very fast spaceship they went
(Even faster where space-time was bent).
    But soon they would learn
    That they couldn't return
To their star 'cause their fuel was all spent.

But before they discovered that fact
They attempted to find the exact
    Location of Stan,
    The unfortunate man
Who was watching some stage actors act.

But why was it Stan that they sought?
'Cause Stan was a great astronaut!
    He'd been to the moon,
    And Mars and Neptune—
Or at least this is what they had thought.

They beamed the man up to their station,
And not for a summer vacation!
    Their ship was obscure
    From Earthlings for sure
On the moon's farther side—good location!

Though something about them was scary,
At first sight they looked quite ordinary,
    'Cause they were "shape-shifters"
    But also shoplifters.
They called themselves Gary and Mary.

When roaming the earth they would steal
All sorts of things they'd conceal,
    And beam those things up
    To their ship for their sup.
They'd cook some strange stuff for their meal.

They really loved things made of metal,
Which they'd melt in a very large kettle.
    They'd eat it with zest
    And then they would rest,
'Cause sleeping made their "stomachs" settle.

On their screen was a view, slightly foggy,
Of Gordon, the dog, slightly soggy.
    In front of his door
    Was a damp carnivore,
And Stan said, "Hey, there sits my doggy!

"Hey guys, that's my dog. Let me go!"
But the aliens simply said, "No!
    You're staying with us.
    Now don't make a fuss!
We're really your friend, not your foe.

"We'll beam your wet dog up here, too.
When dry he'll be part of our crew."
    So in no time at all —
    In his mouth his toy ball —
Gordon was there, it was true!

The aliens called him Flash Gordon
'Cause of old TV shows they'd been hoardin'.
    How many shows?
    God only knows,
But tons of them they'd been recordin'.

Gordon's tail started wagging like mad
As soon as he spotted his "dad."
    As he held his dog near,
    Stan lost all of his fear
Of these beings who seemed not so bad.

When they found they had no more fuel left,
The beings committed a theft:
    Without pandemonium

They stole some plutonium
From earth, and they did it with deft.

To Komondor A they went back.
It was faster than going Amtrak.
    The man and his dog
    Both slept like a log,
But their suitcase they never did pack.

When they woke they were on a strange planet.
With their eyes they attempted to scan it.
    While looking around
    They heard a strange sound
From the voice of the creature who ran it.

They looked at this creature and saw
A blue "wolf" holding up a big paw.
    She was large with long fur.
    A strange feeling did stir
Inside Gordon that put him in awe.

Stan and his dog soon found out
That all kinds of strange wolves roam about.
    So Gordon made friends,
    And hours he spends
Romping till all tuckered out.

They saw that this world was quite nice;
It was almost like some paradise.
    The beings were kind.
    The dog never whined.
Leaving earth was no great sacrifice.

Gordon and Stan remained there
On this world, which had much cleaner air
    Than Earth had before,
    But it started to pour.
When it rains, it sure rains everywhere!

197
AT LEAST HE ALLOWS PETS

I might have to live in a tent,
'Cause my landlord has just raised my rent.
    He'd heard I'd adopted
    A puppy I've opted
To bring home without his consent.

198
THE EURASIER

His loyalty is without measure.
His company is a true pleasure.
    A cross between Chow
    And Wolf-Spitz somehow,
I am talking about the Eurasier.

Pale yellow, grey, black, red, or sand,
His rich coat's rather soft to your hand.
    He'll rarely complain,
    He's easy to train,
He will follow your every command.

He's well suited to family life.
All of your kids and your wife
    Will find him quite affable
    And quite photographable.
He's quiet and causes no strife.

With other dogs very gregarious,
While playing he's often hilarious.
    But don't leave him alone,
    He'll be sad and will moan,
And he'll think you are cruel and barbarious.

199
LET THEM WHINE

At mealtime while eating my food,
They sit there and make me feel rude.
    But when they begin whining
    I just go on dining,
'Cause I'm just a cool laid-back dude!

200
THE KELPIE (WITH "EYES")

A Kelpie's intense, staring eyes
Can a whole flock of sheep mesmerize.
    On the backs he will walk
    Of a tightly bunched flock.
'Twould be no great surprise if he flies!

201
THE VACUUM

When my dogs hear me start the vacuum,
They dodge it and run from the room.
    They look at me, pleading,
    As though I were meting
Out punishment, torture, and doom.

Why do they hate the vacuum?
The sound hurts their ears, I presume;
    For their ears are so keen,
    They can hear a dropped bean
As though it were some sonic boom!

Perhaps if they wear some ear plugs
When I vacuum the floors and the rugs,
   While sucking up fleas,
   They'd be much more at ease,
And our place would not be full of bugs!

202
CRY "HAVOC!" AND LET SLIP
THE DOGS OF WAR

Wearing collars with razor-sharp knives,
Armored dogs made men run for their lives.
   Legs of horses were torn.
   For lives folks did morn.
It was Mastiffs that wore those sharp knives.

Our Mastiffs are gentler these days
Than they were when they made those forays;
   Though when one wants to play,
   Best get out of his way
Or you may find out just what he weighs!

203
GOD FORBID I SHOULD PULL!

Why is my dog lunging ahead?
So I'll slip and then fall on my head?
   He is not being nice;
   I could slip on the ice
And wind up in a hospital bed!

Why is my dog lagging behind?
To make me go out of my mind?

He will sniff and then mark
Every tree in the park.
But, OK, I won't pull — I'll be kind!

204
THE MAN DRESSED IN BROWN

When they spy a large truck on the street,
If it's brown, they might just get a treat.
     If a UPS truck
     Pulls up, they're in luck!
And they race to the door — a dead heat!

When the man dressed in brown's at the door,
They know there's a good treat in store;
     When that guy in khakis
     Starts to feed them cookies,
They just won't stop begging for more!

205
RACING MACHINE

When they run forty miles per hour
You can't help but admire their power.
     When they chase a live bunny
     It's not very funny —
The bunny's fate could be quite dour.

But when chasing mechanical prey
The life of a Greyhound is gray;
     If they don't win the races,
     In most of the cases,
They're killed — quite a big price to pay.

Although owners of champs make big dough,
Their dogs aren't so happy, you know.
    They get just enough care
    To keep chasing that "hare,"
And destroyed if their pace is too slow.

They're treated as though they were plastic,
And what happens to slow ones is drastic.
    Though the tracks are no fun,
    When these fleet dogs do run
The speed they attain is fantastic!

They're faster than any dog known.
In a race this is easily shown.
    This most ancient dog breed
    Holds the record for speed,
Yet will drool like all dogs for a bone.

206
SONYA

My large, lanky mongrel named Sonya
Had recently sniffed some ammonia.
    She started to sneeze,
    She started to wheeze,
And ended up catching pneumonia.

I took her to a good local vet.
I felt kind of nervous, upset,
    And slightly uptight
    And distracted despite
The good doc saying, "Sir, do not fret,

"'Cause we'll just give your dog penicillin
If you want your dog cured and are willin'
    To dish out lots of money.

You think that is funny?
I'd like to get paid — I'm no villain!"

Suddenly things were quite strange:
The dogs in this place all had mange.
    "OK, I will pay,"
    I said in dismay,
"But I don't have too much — just some change."

"No problem, I'll send you a bill,
'Cause I don't want your dog to stay ill.
    You need not pay now …"
    The vet raised an eyebrow
In a way that just gave me a chill!

My dog was then taken from me.
Where they took her I couldn't quite see.
    I ran all around
    Till I heard a faint sound
Like a dog crying, "Please set me free!"

I was searching for such a long while,
It seemed like I'd gone a whole mile!
    The cries were now stronger.
    Each cry lasted longer.
Was this ordeal some sort of trial?

I finally found a glass door
Whence the cries were becoming a roar.
    They had Sonya strapped tight.
    The sight gave me a fright!
My poor doggy was chained to the floor!

She was desperately trying to fight
To get free of the chains and to bite.
    I could no more than stare
    At the mad scene in there.
She was struggling with all of her might.

They had the poor mongrel sedated,
Which made me quite infuriated.

They gave her an injection
Despite my objection.
    Was her life now to be terminated?

"What do you think you are doing!
 Do you like the idea of me suing?"
    I yelled and I screamed
    And the tears even streamed;
I was furious, angry, and stewing.

The scene was becoming too grim;
The light in the room became dim.
    They started to chant.
    (I felt helpless, an ant.)
And they all wore strange hats with a brim.

There were many strange people in there.
They were all dressed in black, I could swear.
    The vet bowed his head.
    Was my Sonya now dead?
It appeared they were gathered in prayer.

In a sweat I awoke—A NIGHTMARE!
I went out on my porch for some air.
    I was followed by Sonya.
    She had no pneumonia,
But, God, the poor dog had no hair!

207

MY BUDDY FROM HARTFORD

I'll tell you a story I heard
From my buddy who lives in Hartford—
    A place in Connecticut
    Where folks have good etiquette
Is where an obscene act occurred:

My friend was enjoying some tea
In a park with some crackers and brie,
    When an Irish Wolfhound
    With no warning came round
And mistook my shocked friend for a tree!

As my buddy described this to me
He was getting quite flushed, I could see.
    As his face became red
    My own shameless dog, Jed,
Just then shamelessly peed on his knee.

When his story was rudely cut short,
My friend's features began to contort.
    He looked down with disdain
    At the warm yellow stain,
And let out an incredulous snort.

Yet my dog wasn't totally through;
Now he aimed for my buddy's left shoe.
    My friend jumped away
    Just in time from the spray,
Which was good, 'cause his shoes looked brand new.

On my dog I should use a squirt gun,
'Cause with *his* he had barely begun!
    Though he didn't quite hit
    His mark, I yelled, "SIT!"
But the damage was already done.

While my friend is a dignified gent,
Out the window his patience just went.
    He growled, "Your vile pet
    Tried to get my shoe wet!
That dog has a singular bent!"

My friend was now so irritated
And so outraged and so aggravated,
    That he started to shout,

His arms flailing about.
He was pretty darn exasperated!

He yelled, "Anything under the sun
That ugly mutt pees on for fun!
    Your big, stupid doggy
    Made my trousers soggy.
He'll lift his leg on ANYONE!"

I said, "Not anyone! That's not true!
Only people he's fond of — like you!
    Though he's making you mad,
    My dog's friendly, not bad!
About nothing you're making ado!

"There are people my dog doesn't like,
Like that wretched, old devil named Mike,
    Whose right leg is a leg,
    But his left one's a peg.
Jed will not on that tyke his leg hike!"

Roared my friend, "He's the only exception!
You know darn well your dog's predilection,
    With not even a bark,
    To go up to and mark
Any fool who will give him affection!

"Yet I wouldn't so much as touch
That despicable creature. He's such
    A nasty brute, sir!
    Tell me, why does that cur
Abuse innocent people so much?"

I said, "My yard's devoid of large plants.
He's no choice but to use people's pants;
    There's not one tree or shrub,
    So there is the rub!
When folks come here, they do take a chance!"

As my mutt who is large and quite furry
Was still eyeing my buddy called Murray,

My friend said, "Good-bye,"
But before my reply
He left in a very big hurry!

(It's been days since my friend and I spoke,
Which is fine, 'cause he's such a mean bloke!
    But poor Jed sure does yearn
    For my friend to return,
'Cause for days he's had no one to soak!)

208
LADDY

There once was a Spaniel named Laddy
Who snatched a large hamburger patty
    From the grill at a party,
    And someone named Marty
Said, "Here, have some mustard, you fatty."

For in truth the dog was quite porcine.
Though his master tried making him lean,
    Wherever they went,
    Some well-meaning gent
Or lady would always be seen

Giving poor Laddy a treat,
Like cookies or biscuits or meat.
    "My dog's on a diet!"
    But they'd say, "Be quiet!
Poor Laddy needs something to eat."

The dog got so fat he looked bloated.
He had one more small bite and exploded!
    He was brought to the vet
    Who said, "Laddy just met
His Maker and it shall be noted

"That this doggy had lots of attention
And enjoyed himself, needless to mention.
    Though too chubby to run,
    At least he had fun —
Though the dog should have practiced abstention."

209
SOMETHING'S OUT THERE

My dog's ears just perked up from a sound.
Outside many things roam around.
    Raccoons, woodchucks, and rats,
    Possums, foxes, and cats.
Through the door he took off with a bound!

I have no idea what the dog found,
For he started to bay like a hound.
    It was clear as a bell,
    From way off in the dell,
Or beyond it, from some higher ground.

I went out on my porch now to peer
Into the night and to hear
    Where his baying came from.
    I sure hope he does come
Back to our house by next year!

Which is actually two days from now.
(I have snow in my driveway to plow.)
    I'd sure like to know
    Where that rascal did go.
I heard a dog bark, "Bow wow wow!"

But that wasn't my dog that did bark.
My dog doesn't bark when it's dark.
    Baying's his thing.

It makes my ears ring.
That strange sound is my doggy's trademark.

My dog has been gone for three days!
Did he choose to hang out with some strays?
    He hasn't come back.
    Tonight is so black!
There's a new moon with feeble light rays.

I'll get my old bugle, blow hard.
Perhaps he will come to the yard.
    I blew it three times.
    He will oftentimes
Respond, 'cause his ears get quite jarred.

I blew it again. But guess what?
I looked down and, why, there was my mutt
    Sitting right by my side!
    I very near cried!
But then laughed, almost split my poor gut!

I'll bet where he was he had fun,
Though the angst had me nearly undone.
    Well, I'll now bring him in,
    Feed my dog his din-din,
And leave not one door open—not one!

210
TITAN

I know a big Mastiff named Titan
Who used to just love to go frighten
    The folks on the street
    That his master would greet,
And their fear he would certainly heighten.

He'd bare the the big teeth in his jaws,
And then jump on those folks with his paws.

People he'd scare
To the point where they'd swear,
    And they'd even get scratched by his claws.

So Titan was taken away.
His life now looked bleak and quite gray.
    He was brought to the pound,
    His sorrow profound.
They would kill the poor dog any day.

But the day Titan was to be taken
To the death room a fellow named Macon
    Comes in and then buys
    The Mastiff who sighs
With relief, for the dog was quite shaken.

Macon trained Titan so well,
It's almost like some broken spell!
    Titan now licks
    Your face and does tricks.
He's now a sweet dog—you can tell.

211
ROLL OVER

My Corgi, on cue, will roll over.
He'll do it for food that's left over.
    He'll give you his paw.
    (Don't get scratched by his claw!)
And if given the chance, he'll take over!

212
QUIET!

They bark at the girls and the boys,
And they even will bark at their toys.
    We'll probably get
    Evicted I'll bet
If my mutts don't stop making that noise.

213
MY TWO MUTTS

Whereas one dog likes chasing the crows,
The other likes grabbing my clothes.
    Though they play different games,
    And they have different names,
They're one with the human they chose.

214
TABLE TENNIS

My friend who arrived from Hong Kong
Tripped on my dog's favorite Kong.
    He was pretty darned pissed
    'Cause he injured his wrist.
But he still whipped my butt in Ping-Pong!

215
FOOD FOR THOUGHT

Though you thought it alarming and gory
When your dog caught that muskrat, his quarry,
    What is far more alarming
    Is factory farming—
The source of dog food. End of story.

216
IN THE PET STORE

My puppy just grabbed a pig's ear
From the pet store before I could see 'er.
    She chewed it so fast,
    She did not make it last.
It was gone by the time I got near.

217
THE STRANGER

The man dogged us down the sidewalk.
I kept walking, did not want to balk.
    Though I knew not his reason,
    He was not me pleasin',
So I stopped and then picked up a rock.

I entrusted the dog I was with
To scare him so he'd leave us forthwith.
    So in spite of my fear
    I let him come near,
But the stranger said, "My name is Smith.

"I tried to catch up with you all
'Cause I saw your dog take my baseball."
　　And my dog I called Keith
　　Had that ball in his teeth,
And I suddenly felt rather small!

218
NO DOGS ALLOWED

No Dogs Allowed in This Place.
Those words put a frown on my face.
　　For dogs aren't as lazy
　　Or warlike or crazy
As our egotistical race!

219
THE "PURE" BREEDS' PROLOGUE

While some say a mutt is a cur,
Others would call that a slur.
　　The original dog,
　　The "pure" breeds' prologue,
Was the mutt whom all "pures" wish they were!

220
NO DIGGING AROUND!

A dog who was some kind of hound
Was arrested for "digging around."
　　But while sitting in jail
　　The dog wagged his tail,
So that hound they did no more impound.

221
SHARING

I was sharing a warm hot dog bun
With my son and my cute honeybun,
When along came our dog
From out of a fog.
It was obvious he wanted one!

222
PICK THAT TICK OFF QUICK, RICK!

Your dog's ear has a sickening smell?
Does the smell smell like some smell from hell?
If the odor's unpleasant
A tick may be present.
Don't let that gross bug in there dwell!

223
CHIP AND DALE

Chip is a Bulldog, quite strong.
He's ugly! His canines are long!
Yet Chip is so chummy
You can rub his big tummy,
And with people and dogs gets along.

Dale is a Yorkie, quite tiny.
She's cute with long fur, sleek and shiny.
Yet who would think
Her breath does stink?
(She also will nip and is whiny.)

224

COWEL MAKES HIM HOWL

When I put on some music by Cowel,
My dog will just sit there and howl.
    I tell him to hush,
    I tell him to shush,
But finally throw in the towel.

225

SHE SAW THE LIGHT

A pup with poor eyesight named Spider,
Burnt her poor, little nose on Steve's lighter:
    Steve had just lit the light
    When the pup tried to bite
His white sleeve, which seemed suddenly brighter!

226

WHAT'S NEXT?

Dogs for hunting and chasing and war;
Dogs for guarding and herding and more—
    All of those breeds
    We have made for our needs.
What else might we yet have in store?

A birdlike and winged sort of dog?
Who, with laser beam eyes, sees through fog?
    It might sight and then bite
    Another in flight.
There could be a dogfight above Prague!

Or perhaps fishlike canines with fins
And thousands of scales on their skins.
    They won't need a dog dish
    When they eat the dogfish,
Though with whales they might have some run-ins!

227

THE IDEAL SITUATION

I think what's really ideal
Is a dog off the leash that will heel.
    You can walk at your pace,
    And go most any place.
That thought has a certain appeal.

228

THE BIG BULL AND THE BRAVE DOG

(If you're squeamish of things that are gory
Then skip over the following story.
Go on to the next
Poem in the text,
'Cause reading this ain't mandatory.)

The farmer was turning his back
Toward the bull, whose big nose was jet black.
    The bull, which was large,
    Decided to charge,
And he did that poor farmer attack.

That two-thousand-pound beast, muscle-bound,
Had the farmer pinned right to the ground.
    The farmer, who reckoned

He'd die in a second,
Just then saw his dog come around.

With sharp hooves, the bull started to rake
The man's back, whose ribs started to break.
    Now running full speed,
    The dog did intercede —
Risked his own life for his master's sake.

He charged and then leapt off his toes,
And bit the bull's ears and his nose.
    (Thought the dog's grateful master,
    When saved from disaster,
That sure is a brave dog I chose!)

Though the pain in his ribs was intense,
The farmer crawled under a fence.
    His dog quickly ran
    To the house of the man
To alert the man's wife (which made sense).

Although never permitted inside,
He decided to put rules aside.
    He found her in bed,
    And without delay led
The stunned woman to her husband's side.

The man was so horribly hurt
That his wife simply had to avert
    Her shocked, helpless eyes
    When she noticed the size
Of his wounds as he lay in the dirt.

But the farmer was tough, didn't die,
And recovered quite well by and by.
    The dog can now come
    In their house (at least some),
And he romps in the dell that's near by.

*Note: This poem is based loosely on the true story of Bailey, the
chocolate Labrador and Chesapeake Bay Retriever mix, who
was named the 1996 Ken-L Ration Dog Hero of the Year for
saving his master's life from a raging bull.*

229
FOUND THE SPOT!

When you scratch my dog's neck on the side,
The joy on his face he can't hide.
    If you find the "right spot"
    His back leg starts to trot—
For a flea on his foot quite a ride!

230
DAILY ROUTINE

If your dog has a daily routine,
Like a walk twice a day, he'll stay lean;
    He'll be very content,
    For his day was well spent.
He'll be tranquil, relaxed, and serene.

231
MISCHIEVOUS STUNTS

My dog's done some mischievous stunts,
Like the time that he ran away once
    With a little girl's panties
    While staying at her aunties—
But he brought them back. He's no dunce!

232
WOLF DEN

A wolf makes her home in the earth
So she'll have a nice place to give birth.
    She really can dig!
    Her den is quite big,
And more comfy than a box from Woolworth.

233
DOGS THAT HEEL AND DOGS THAT FEEL

Shows are for dogs that have money,
But my mongrels don't think that's so funny.
    Though my mutts can't compete
    With the show ring elite,
Their wet kisses are sweeter than honey!

234
SEEING EYE

My guide dog is truly a must,
A creature I can't help but trust.
    When he's walking beside me,
    And working to guide me,
The world doesn't seem so unjust.

When my dog and I stride down the street,
Our teamwork just cannot be beat!
    We are really one creature
    With a curious feature:
Two heads, four keen ears, and six feet!

235
A CONSIDERATE NEIGHBOR

That guy's lawn mower sure makes some noise!
And his Harley he rides with the boys.
　　But what I don't yet get
　　Is he won't let his pet
Even bark — thinks his street it annoys!

236
ELEGY FOR LAIKA

As bright as a small glowing ember,
On the third of the month of November
　　In the year fifty-seven
　　A dog went to heaven
Aboard Sputnik Two. You remember?

In humans she put all her trust.
From her cabin she heard engines thrust.
　　She was hurled into space
　　(For a dog a strange place!)
And died there, her body now dust.

The rocket flew straight as an arrow,
Yet her pressurized room was so narrow
　　She could not move enough
　　To scratch her own scruff!
(It was even too small for a sparrow!)

While in orbit for seven whole days,
She received no affection or praise.
　　Then they put her to sleep —
　　Did anyone weep? —
Like the pounds do to thousands of strays.

149

Where her soul is now no one does know,
But I'll bet there is no ice or snow.
    Her spirit's up there
    Where there's not too much air.
To that martyr much homage we owe.

Note: On November 3, 1957, the Soviet Union launched a dog into space aboard **Sputnik 2.** *Her name was Laika, which means "barker" in Russian. She was the first living creature in space. There was no way to return Laika to earth, so she died in space about a week after the launch. The satellite itself remained in orbit 162 days.*

237
IN TROUBLE

There once was a dog from Nantucket
Who got his head stuck in a bucket.
    He couldn't get out
    And he hadn't a doubt
That if there too long he'd "kick the bucket."

238
THE DOG PARK

When the dogs in the dog park run free,
They have a great time—a big spree!
    When they play with each other
    Like sister and brother,
It's something you truly must see!

What I think is a really cool sight
Is a dog catching Frisbees in flight.
    But when *all* the dogs play,
    They're as carefree and gay
And as bright as a kite in sunlight!

239
SCARCE IMPROVEMENT

They wanted the ears of that pup
To be stiff and be pointing straight up.
    So his ears they did crop.
    His cute tail they did lop.
And so now the poor pup is SCREWED UP!

240
"CLAIR DE LUNE" AIN'T THIS DOG'S TUNE

In my town lives a curious stray
Who often will plaintively bay,
    But not at the moon.
    He does it at noon.
"Clair de *Noon*" is his tune, I would say.

Whereas humans are mostly diurnal,
Canines are largely nocturnal.
    So that dog's a bit "funny"
    To bay when it's sunny.
(He's mentioned in some doggie journal.)

241
LET HIM BE NEAR

For our dogs we're a good substitute
Of a wolf pack without much dispute.
    So let him be near,
    For he may disappear
If kept out like some kind of a brute.

242
BLAND BUT CONVENIENT

Kibble is quite a bland diet.
Don't believe me? Then why don't *you* try it?
    Though my dog can do fine on
    The fare that I dine on,
It's just for convenience I buy it.

243
A PET VIGNETTE

He often sneaks away without a trace;
For days he's gone if on a rabbit chase.
Always creatures he's pursuing;
Thinks that leashes are for chewing;
Things he tears have been accruing;
Heels with zero grace,
Pulls like it's a race,
Makes me go *his* pace …
Yet there's one small thing he does
That lets me know he knows his place:
He loves to lick my face!

244
A SMART DOG

I have a smart Golden Retriever.
For new tricks he is one eager beaver!
    He goes to dog school.
    He will not even drool—
You believe that?—you could not be naiver!

245
LITTLE BANDITOS

A pack of Chihuahuas from Chiapas
Last Saturday managed to stop us
    From eating our lunch
    After one spilled our punch,
And the others ran off with our tapas.

246
SHE CAN'T HELP IT, POOR THING

When my dog hears but one corn chip drop,
Or soup boiling on the stove top,
    She'll be waiting right there
    Near my foot (only fair!),
But her drool I will then have to mop!

247
WHAT IS HE THINKING?

With a soccer ball he's fascinated.
My dog plays with it till it's deflated,
    Which doesn't take long,
    For his jaws are so strong,
From his teeth it gets quite perforated!

I then kick that poor ball really hard,
And he'll chase it full speed down the yard.
    With his canines he grabs it
    And shakes it and stabs it.
That ball becomes punctured and scarred.

Yet the thing that his eye teeth are shrinking
And tearing and deep into sinking,
    Perhaps in his mind
    Is some very strange kind
Of a creature — is that what he's thinking?

Though he knows it is not a muskrat,
Woodchuck, opossum, or cat,
    He knows not what it is,
    But believes it is his —
Till it's wholly deflated and flat!

248
WET SPOT

Are you suggesting that my little Pug
Caused that wet spot you see on your rug?
    Guess what? It was you!
    You deserve a loud boo!
'Cause you just spilled some beer from your mug!

249
ANYTHING FOR CHEESE!

I know of a cute Irish Setter
Who will give you her paw when you pet 'er.
    She'll sit on command
    And eat out of your hand
If it holds a small tidbit of cheddar.

250
DINNER

A she-wolf will regurgitate
Meat for her cubs who await
    A nutrient rich
    Dinner for which
They won't even need a hotplate!

251
MY NEW PUPPY

This cute little pup yesterday
Ran up to me wanting to play.
    But before he could roam
    I brought him right home.
So now he's no longer a stray.

The pup chewed up four shoes by now.
I replaced them and then made a vow:
    To keep things from reach,
    And to make time to teach
Him to chew only things I allow.

But the puppy, in lieu of a shoe,
Munched a container of glue.
    With his jaws now glued shut,
    When he barks, the poor mutt,
Sounds just like a broken kazoo!

The way that he eats is quite neat!
It's truly a delicate feat:
    Through straws in his jaws,
    Which he holds with his paws,
He eats soup and raw eggs (but no meat).

252
GOOD GARBAGE

Of good garbage there's rarely a lack,
So I love to hang out by the back
     Of the dumpster of trash —
     It's an excellent cache
Of good spoiled food for a snack!

But my master gets very upset,
Believing his wonderful pet
     From the stuff will get ill
     And he'll have a vet bill.
He gets pretty darn peeved and will fret.

The dumpster is also a place
Where squirrels and birds feed their face.
     They climb in for stale bread.
     (Some are fat and well fed.)
So I dash to the trash just in case.

Who knows what small creatures might feed
In that can? So I run there full speed!
     Though they're just too darn fast,
     I still have a blast,
'Cause it keeps me in great shape indeed!

253
SOME THINGS A DOG CAN'T PASS OVER

The dog had just ruined the Seder!
In the matzos she left a big crater.
     Poor, hungry Sable
     Had jumped on the table —
She just couldn't wait until later.

254
I WANT ABSOLUTE OBEDIENCE

A dogmatic dog owner from Gloucester
Had lost his poor dog 'cause he'd bossed 'er.
    When he forced her to sit,
    The scared dog turned and bit—
Out the window the tyrant then tossed 'er.

She went far away from that man—
She made tracks, she hightailed it, she ran,
    She skedaddled, she split,
    And nearly got hit
When she ran right in front of a van.

But it swerved and just missed the dog's head.
From the van stepped a youngster named Fred.
    Cried the lad, "Listen, Dad,
    I want a dog bad!"
(The dog's now asleep in Fred's bed.)

255
THE TITLE OF THIS ONE SLIPPED MY MIND

Though my dogs are now very well trained,
And some worldly experience gained,
    Have been many places
    And put through their paces,
Their master is still scatterbrained!

256
WHO OWNS WHOM?

From a pet store I got him a bone.
From an ice cream shop he got a cone.
    He got his way,
    And I got to pay
For that mutt I supposedly own!

257
A DOGGY NAMED CAT

There once was a doggy named Cat
Who had very short legs and was fat.
    Like a cat she would purr
    And had very long fur.
Folks adored that strange doggy named Cat.

Cat had a master named Dog
Who frequently sat on a log.
    Cat would then nap
    And purr on Dog's lap
While her master would watch joggers jog.

Since Cat was a dog she would chase
Felines all over the place.
    They would let her come near,
    For those cats had no fear,
And would scratch that poor dog in the face!

One day while Cat rode in Dog's car
On the way to the town's reservoir,
    She stuck out her snout
    And looked all about.
Her sharp little eyes could see far!

Cat saw a cat and jumped out,
On hitting the pavement passed out,
  Then passed away.
  That Sunday was gray.
Dog was quite sad and did pout.

The folks in that town miss that creature
With the curious feline-like feature.
  Now Dog sits alone,
  And sometimes will moan,
Watching joggers jog by from a bleacher.

(But this story need not have been sad.
For if Dog's little catlike comrade
  Had a seat belt, that mutt
  Would have kept her big butt
In the car, and now Dog would be glad.)

258
CAUGHT RED-HANDED!

A man who was rather unfeeling
Was nabbed and arrested for stealing
  A big St. Bernard
  From the St. Bernard's yard.
To a judge he will soon be appealing!

259
ON CUE

On cue my Dalmatian will spin,
And he does it with such a big grin,
    You can see his big smile
    From nearly a mile,
Like sunlight reflecting off tin!

On cue my Dalmatian will crawl!
He also likes fetching a ball.
    He'll give a "high five,"
    And that ain't no jive!
And *sometimes* he'll come when I call.

260
GYPSY

An Australian Shepherd named Gypsy
Used to herd all the kids in Poughkeepsie,
    Till one little kid
    Who called himself Sid
Gave her stout and she got rather tipsy.

While drunk, she was not a good herder.
Just standing up felt like murder.
    So she slept for ten hours,
    Regained all her powers,
And suddenly things got absurder.

The next day the dog searched all about,
Found those kids and then herded them out
    Of town. And they never
    Were seen again, ever.
(Perhaps she just wanted more stout.)

261
TEETHING

If your pup chews your shoe it's expected.
If you punish her she'll feel dejected.
 Give her a toy,
 One she'll enjoy,
So her chewing will be redirected.

262
YOUR DOG

Whether black, brown, red, yellow, or white,
Or medium, heavy, or light;
 Regardless of size
 Or breed, I'd surmise
That your dog makes your days and nights bright.

263
FRAMED!

A coyote who lived in the sticks
Had eaten some small baby chicks.
 But a mongrel was blamed.
 That poor doggy was framed,
And he's now in a bit of a fix!

264
A BLIMP IN THE SKY

My dog saw a blimp in the sky.
He watched it as it floated by.
    Perhaps he inferred
    It was some GIANT BIRD.
That object did him mystify.

Was that big, swollen blob a HUGE TICK
That would burst from just one good hard kick?
    (His keen hunter's eyes,
    On which my dog relies,
Were, on him, surely playing a trick!)

Perhaps it's a creature quite rare:
A gigantic "OPOSSUM-WHALE-BEAR,"
    So bloated and light,
    With one jump it's in flight!
(At the thought my dog raised his short hair!)

Whatever it was, it was FAT! —
Far more than the WORLD'S FATTEST RAT!
    What could that "thing" eat?
    Does the "thing" live on meat? —
Carnivorous, just like a cat?

My dog, who's a speedy Greyhound,
Can run past twenty cats in one bound!
    But that monster up there
    At which my dog did stare …
How fast would it run on the ground?

Where will that behemoth alight
From its great, lofty, staggering height?
    Perhaps in a meadow
    Of palm and palmetto,
Later today or tonight.

At that blimp he kept staring and staring.
It was not in the least my dog scaring.
    In fact, I dare think,
    If, to earth, it dare sink,
With big teeth, its soft "flesh," he'd be tearing!

265
BECAUSE SHE WAS ABLE

There once was a doggy named Mocha
Who loved to watch people play "poka."
    She'd jump on the table,
    Because she was ABLE,
And mess up the cards — what a "joka!"

But one day her crazed master, insane,
Caused poor Mocha to suffer a pain.
    "Since you're ABLE to jump,
    With my CANE, your big rump
I shall strike, so you shan't jump again!"

So Mocha, though ABLE, did not
Mess the cards up again 'cause that swat
    She received from that CANE
    Left a mark on her brain,
And feared she might, next time, get shot!

266
IF YOU'RE KIND, SHE WILL MIND

If your dog doesn't listen, don't beat 'er!
Or she'll then only come when you feed 'er.
    Have her sit, stay, or stand,
    Or lie down on command.
Then pet 'er or hug 'er or treat 'er.

267
PAUSE FOR CLAWS

You must trim your doggy's long claws!
I advise you to do this because
    When he walks his nails click.
    But stay clear of the quick,
Or he won't like you handling his paws!

268
CURED!

There was a young lady named Mia,
Who, of dogs, had a horrible fear.
    But while at her friend's place
    His big mutt licked her face!
Which made Mia's big fear disappear.

269
TRAIN 'ER

If she's punished for making a mess,
For your pup, it would only cause stress.
    Would it not be humaner
    To simply go train 'er?
When good give her treats and say, "YES!"

270
FEAR (IN THE STYLE OF LEAR)

There was an old man of Tangier
With a deep pathological fear
    Of dogs. But guess what …
    A very large mutt
Ate that old man of Tangier!

271
STRESSED OUT PUP

Does your doggy act way too stressed out?
Does he spin, chase his tail, run about?
    If your dog's hyperactive
    He should be more active:
From exercise he'll be worn out.

Give him agility training.
On his energy it will be draining.
    Have him go run.
    He'll have lots of fun,
Or play Frisbee—it's quite entertaining!

Maybe soft music just play
To calm your dog during the day.
    If you've bought some Prozac
    Then just bring it right back!
'Cause music's a far better way.

When your doggy is sleeping at night
You can turn on a pleasing blue light.
    A light bulb that's blue
    Is relaxing, it's true.
Will it make your dog calm? It just might!

You can get calming herbs from your vet,
In a formula known as Calm Pet.
    These herbs will relax
    Your dog so he acts
Calm with a better mindset.

Here is another good plan:
There's a chemical called tryptophan.
    Milk has this stuff.
    It has just enough.
Warm up the milk in a pan.

Give him just one quarter cup
Twice a day — he will lap it right up.
    It will calm him right down
    So he won't be a clown
Like some frenzied and hyper young pup.

272
(OR TRY A HEAD HALTER
AS A "HALTERNATIVE")

When I see a dog wearing a prong
Collar, I think it is wrong.
    Why not just *train*
    The dog to refrain
From dragging his handler along?

273

YOU SUPPOSE HE KNOWS I CHOSE
HIS PROSE FOR LUNCH?
WONDERS THE PUP
'BOUT HIS MASTER NAMED KRUP

Though his drawings and poems were nutritious,
His prose was a lot more delicious!
    Those big pages had crunch.
    They were such fun to munch!
Though my hunch is he'll soon be suspicious.

274

A FLY FLEW BY

Dog said, "I'll catch you, you fly!"
Fly said, "I dare you, go try!"
    Dog jumped up so darn fast
    Fly barely flew past,
Saying, "Next time try harder! Goodbye!"

275

A WARM FEELING

Boy looked at his dog who was old,
And asked, "Why is your nose wet and cold?"
    The dog pressed his muzzle
    'Gainst Boy's leg to nuzzle.
Thought Boy, *Wouldn't trade you for gold!*

276
CLOROPHYLLED

Unlike cats which are truly carnivorous,
The Lord made our doggy omnivorous.
    He not only eats meat,
    But loves grass which tastes sweet.
But please Lord, from his vomit, deliver us!

277
GRASS IN NANTUCKET

A dog who ate grass in Nantucket
Felt a powerful urge to upchuck it.
    She threw up so much grass,
    'Twas a giant, green mass—
But that's better than kicking the bucket!

278
READ PAT'S BOOK AND
GIVE YOUR DOG A PAT

If your dog won't obey you, don't kill 'er!
Instead read the book by Pat Miller.
    In place of choke chaining
    Try positive training.
With joy your new method will fill 'er!

279
THE CATALYST

I knew a dog from Cincinnati
Who was mangy, bedraggled, and ratty.
    She lived on the street,
    Ate old bones, rotten meat,
Fought with dogs and chased cats—what a bratty!

She sure did not look like a winner;
She looked anything but "a dog's dinner!"
    She was homely and strange,
    Most likely had mange,
And could not have been any thinner.

Folks did not like that flea-bitten cur.
They kicked and threw big sticks at her.
    It was not very nice.
    She lived mostly on mice
And trash. But a change did occur:

She stumbled on Boy who was eight.
Upon bringing her home Boy did rate
    His new mutt as the best
    Thing he'd ever possessed!
That first evening they both stayed up late.

He gave her a bath. She got clean.
She ate well and no longer looked lean.
    She loved that young boy,
    Gave him much joy,
And was happy, content, and serene,

Till Boy's father got angry one day
About something Boy's mother did say.
    Full of stout, he did shout,
    And then threw the dog out
Of the second floor window the way

A man hurls a stick or a brick.
Thought Boy, *That sure was a mean trick!*
    Boy ran outside,
    Saw his dog and then cried,
And felt terribly saddened and sick.

Though she had a bad cut on her ear,
The dog's injuries weren't that severe.
    Dismayed at his father,
    Boy wouldn't bother
Coming back home — that was clear.

He could not really understand why
His father was such mean guy.
    So Boy ran away.
    He was too scared to stay
In that house, for his dog may well die!

About running the kid felt no shame.
Can you truly the poor youngster blame?
    From locale to locale
    He went with his pal.
Surviving was their only aim.

They joined up with some hoods in the woods
Who stole from the town many goods,
    Such as food, guns, and clothes;
    How they did, no one knows.
Those bandits missed few neighborhoods.

An unspoken contract they drew up.
Boy and Dog were now larcenists. Yup!
    But when those men drank whisky,
    Boy felt it too risky
To stay there. His life they'd screw up!

He did not want to be with those men,
So Boy began running again.
    He did not want to rob.

He wanted a job,
Which he got—a big turning point then.

Well, what kind of work did he take?
Odd jobs where good dough he did make.
    He cat and dog sat—
    Nothing to sneeze at!—
And mowed lawns till his muscles did ache.

It's been eight years since finding his pet.
In establishments people would let
    Dog come inside.
    Boy felt much pride
'Bout his dog, which was never a threat.

Every day the two buddies would play.
Boy threw sticks for the old, former stray.
    Each morning they'd stretch,
    And go out and play fetch.
There was never a day that was gray.

From his home, Boy was now very far.
He had recently bought a used car,
    Was renting a pad—
    A bit cramped but not bad—
And was learning to play the guitar.

Music became His Main Thing,
And Dog enjoyed hearing Boy sing.
    That teen had a bent,
    A gift, and had spent
Much time practicing all through the spring.

Then Boy took his dog on the road.
He performed everywhere till it snowed.
    It was now wintertime
    And he thought now's the time
To write a great poem—an ode.

"About dogs I will write. It will rhyme."
The poem he composed was sublime!

'Bout dogs like Ol' Yeller,
'Twas a best seller—
A tale about dogs in their prime.

But *Boy's* dog was truly the star
In his subsequent work: a memoir.
She was now "ninety-nine,"
And feeling just fine.
Well, that's it for my yarn. Au revoir!

280
GETTING RID OF SMELLY KELLY

My dog rolls on objects so rotten,
The smell is not quickly forgotten.
My mongrel named Kelly
Is often so smelly,
Of late I've been schemin' and plottin'

To get rid of that noisome old cur,
For I can't stand the smell of her fur!
To my neighbors I say
I shall give her away.
With my sentiments they all concur.

But my stinking malodorous mutt
Is not cute enough. Anything but!
She's friendly however,
But nobody ever
Pets her. The smell turns their gut.

Folks cringe when she crosses their path,
Yet she won't let me give her a bath.
When we go for a walk,
Passers-by gawk,
And I feel like a sociopath!

To a hydrant I'll tie the dog up.
Will the dog warden then pick her up?
    I really do pray
    She'll be taken away.
If not I'll go crazy, crack up!

She's been chained to that hydrant a week.
Things are now looking quite bleak.
    She's been starting to howl,
    But smells no less foul.
That mongrel of mine still does reek.

So I went to that foul-smelling beast,
And unchained her. The dog was released.
    I then grabbed a hose.
    She got washed tail to nose.
And directly her odor decreased!

But before she was dry that dog went
Roaming, and hours she spent
    Romping in grime
    And in filth, muck, and slime;
And much anguish I then underwent.

I called, but on hearing my words,
She wolfed down twenty tasty goose turds.
    With my gun I then shot
    The dog on the spot.
Now she is food for the birds!

Relax! I have merely been jokin',
And at Kelly some fun I've been pokin'.
    When I showed her this rhyme,
    She said it is time
To "quit all this nonsense!" Well spoken!

281
A TASTE FOR MOLES

A hungry, old hunter's dog, Bert,
Had been digging a hole in the dirt
    When way deep in the hole
    Bert discovered a mole,
Who cried, "Please put me down. Your teeth hurt!"

Said the dog, "You look great for desert!
My stomach juices will convert
    Your small bod into food.
    I'll be in a good mood."
This sure put the mole on high alert!

Just before the dog ate the poor thing,
A bird snatched the poor thing on the wing.
    A hunter caught sight
    Of the bird while in flight,
And the blast from his gun sure did ring!

Falling to earth was a shock.
The mole feared she might need a "mole doc."
    She dug under a mound,
    As big Bert, the old hound,
Away with that dead bird did walk.

The small mole was relieved and exclaimed,
"I'm sure glad that I haven't been maimed!"
    She went back to her burrow
    In the town of Marlborough,
And thought, *That dog cannot be blamed.*

I suppose he just needed a meal.
Moles must to dog's taste buds appeal.
    Then she snatched up a bug
    In the hole she had dug,
While old Bert by the hunter did heel.

As the two strode away with their prize,
The dog gazed at the prize with keen eyes.
    Though at birds he does stare,
    He's fed dog food. Not fair!
About moles Bert did now fantasize.

The next day, in their yard, he did dig
Twenty holes, and he made them all big.
    Bert had not much regard
    For his master's backyard,
And the hunter went nuts—flipped his wig!

While some treatment the man underwent,
To a farm the old hound dog was sent.
    In the big ol' cornfield
    Lots of moles were revealed.
Bert had moles to his old heart's content!

But he ate so darn many that May,
He lay in the hay a whole day.
    With a big bellyache,
    In the sun he did bake,
And did never, with moles, again play!

282
UNDETERRED

A tough dog who stole everyone's lunches,
When hit, simply rolled with the punches,
    Till a black belt named Rick
    Gave that dog such a kick,
He now *hides* while their lunches he munches.

283
PLAYING

I'll wag my tail, do a play-bow.
I want to play. Bow wow wow!
 See my play-face?
 Come on! Let's have a chase!
Who put that tree there? Ow! Ow! Ow!

284
THE MOST IMPORTANT BEHAVIOR

I think it's a good rule of thumb
To teach your new puppy to come;
 You'll keep him from harm,
 And he'll have lots of charm
As the good dog he'll therefore become.

285
SQUIRRELS ON THE BRAIN

When those squirrels they stalk and pursue,
I can call my two mutts till I'm blue!
 While those rodents they tree,
 They don't listen to me.
Now what am I going to do?

Every day with good food they are fed;
They each have their own comfy dog bed.
 I think you'll concede
 They have good lives indeed,
But I fear I'm in over my head.

So I guess I'll just give them away.
When I do it will be a sad day —
    Not for me, but for them.
    Can you really condemn
My feelings? They just don't obey!

You're a trainer? Well, what do you say?
I should keep them on leashes? OK.
    Teach them simple commands?
    Feed them out of my hands?
Take them both to dog school? Don't delay?

Eight whole weeks have gone by since that talk.
Every day on a leash they now walk.
    They do all kinds of tricks;
    They even fetch sticks.
Yet, when loose, they still squirrels do stalk!

To the pound I'll now give those dogs up.
I have made up my mind. It's true. Yup!
    I'm just pulling your leg!
    Look! They've come now to beg.
I forgot: it's now time for their sup!

286
SPIKE

Spike is a dog that I like,
Whose handler's my big brother, Ike.
    They both have brown hair,
    They both sniff the air,
And when barking, sound truly alike.

When Ike picked up Spike from the pound
She was quite overjoyed to be found.
    Of each other they're fond;

They have such a strong bond,
I would just have to call it profound!

I've accompanied them everywhere:
To Bel Air, Delaware, and Times Square;
    In stores and cafes,
        At concerts and plays,
And they often will share the same chair.

Spike has a mischievous smile,
She's friendly and brave and agile.
    Eager to please,
        Even more so for cheese,
She'll hike with Ike mile after mile.

When Ike takes a hike by the dike,
Climbs a mountain, or rides on his bike,
    Spike tags along
        All day or night long.
She's a very game four-legged tyke.

If Ike's feeling sick or depressed
Or stressed or not feeling his best,
    Spike will lick his big nose
        (But never his toes).
'Bout her empathy, I am impressed!

When the neighborhood children come by,
Spike wags her tail to say, "Hi!"
    Since Spike has no fears,
        When they pull on her ears,
She will lick all their noses (or try).

Her muscular body is lean
And her smooth, silky fur has a sheen.
    Her ears are uncropped,
        Her tail is unlopped.
And she looks like a fighting machine—

For Spike is an APBT.*
I've seen that dog climb up a tree!

(Teddy Roosevelt had one,
And not such a bad one —
That dog was as sweet as can be!)

Spike and Ike and myself (I am Mike)
Were once walking along the turnpike,
    When a man with a gun
    Said, "Come over here, son!"
And Spike wagged her tail, ladylike!

'Twas twilight, the air thick with fog.
He did not, at first, see the brown dog;
    But when moonbeams, quite pale,
    Revealed Spike's waggly tail,
He wheeled round and away he did jog!

There was one other time when a stranger
With a gun came, and we were in danger.
    The thug wanted money.
    It wasn't too funny,
'Cause Spike was asleep in the manger.

He came ambling towards us from across
The horse yard and said, "Hi, I'm Ross.
    Hand over your bread,
    Or you'll shortly be dead!"
We were stunned, and for words, at a loss.

But Spike took one look at that crook,
And did not like his manner or look.
    At the gunman she leapt,
    For she's very adept
At telling a crook from a schnook.

Now Spike was not playing around!
Without any warning or sound
    She grabbed his gun hand
    With her teeth. It was grand!
He fell backwards and hit the hard ground.

While his hand she held fast in her jaws
And stood on his chest with her paws,
    My brother, with speed,
    Grabbed the gun — guaranteed
To stop any thug, give him pause!

Astonished, astounded, surprised,
The man understood, realized,
    That he'll no longer steal;
    To a judge he'll appeal.
(For his actions he was penalized.)

Spike's like *Our Gang's* Pete the Pup.
In a contest she'll never give up.
    She competes in weight pulls
    With other Pit Bulls.
Last Sunday she was runner-up!

*American Pit Bull Terrier

287
FLUFFY'S NEW "COLLAR"

Fluffy, a dog from Nantucket,
Had got her head stuck in a bucket.
    Thought the dog, *I'll be dammed,*
    For my head is so jammed,
I should not in this bucket have stuck it!

That pail had a very strange form.
It didn't conform to the norm:
    Its designer had gall,
    For its top was too small.
It was dark in that space and too warm.

Of that pail she just couldn't get free —
Shook her head and slammed into a tree;
    She waggled and whirled

And twisted and twirled,
Yet she couldn't her pail-prison flee.

How long could her head stay in there
Before it used up all the air?
    Thought uncomfortable Fluffy,
    It's sure getting stuffy.
That thought gave poor Fluffy a scare.

The air's getting thin and so stale,
Thought Fluffy, and started to wail.
    Must get out of this place!
    It's contusing my face.
And I hope no one steps on my tail!

Passersby, seeing her plight,
Thought, *My Lord, what a terrible sight!*
    Those folks were aghast,
    But they had to act fast,
For her chance of surviving was slight.

Two strong men came and used all their might.
They began when the sun was still bright;
    One grabbed the dog's tail,
    The other the pail,
And they pulled through the day and all night.

At times they could hear a faint wailing.
Much effort this thing was entailing;
    Yet those men wouldn't quit.
    They used muscle and grit,
For they wanted to see an unveiling!

Poor Fluffy just wanted to shout,
"What's taking so long? Get me out!
    It is just pure bad luck
    I'm so horribly stuck—
And the pressure's still hurting my snout!"

In the dark Fluffy started to dream;
Now the whole world around her did seem

Engulfed by an ocean —
What a queer notion —
And through it, a distant light beam;

On the light beam was riding her master,
Flying towards her, now faster and faster.
    He said, "There is my pup!"
    She yelled, "Stop! Pick me up!"
But instead, he just waved and flew past 'er …

After three days those men were dog-tired
And fatigued and pooped out and perspired.
    So some other folks came,
    With a much different aim —
A plan that was truly inspired:

They used a huge can opener
To "open" the bucket. Yes sir!
    The pail started to creak
    And to vibrate and squeak,
And the hoped-for event did occur!

Fluffy's tail began wagging like mad,
Even while she felt wobbly and bad.
    'Cause her nose was exposed —
    No longer enclosed
In that bucket — and Fluffy was glad.

The people were happy, they were!
'Cause they'd saved the poor, innocent cur
    From a horrible fate.
    Can you relate?
It's amazing what Fluff did endure.

Her whole head was revealed before long.
And though weak, the dog did get along
    Fairly well I would say;
    She could eat, drink, and play,
But when bumped, made a noise like a gong!

For she still wore the bucket's steel shell
Round her neck, and it clanged like a bell.
    She could not turn her head—
    It felt heavy, like lead,
And she hit things and stumbled and fell.

Her new "collar" of galvanized steel,
When struck made a sonorous peal;
    A metallic lamp shade—
    For Fluff's neck, tailor-made—
It made tones like a huge glockenspiel!

But when Fluff had an itch on her neck,
She'd no choice but to think, *What the heck!*
    My hind foot can't get past
    This metallic "neck-cast."
Flustered Fluff was becoming a wreck.

A musician of fame and renown,
Fluff's master had been out of town.
    He'd been the main guest
    At a famous jazz fest,
And he'd also been gigging aroun'.

After playing a concert in Rome,
Fluff's master, at last, came back home;
    Upon seeing his mutt,
    The musician cried, "What!"
But then thought, *We could play in Stockholm.*

He said, "Fluffy, you'll do some neat tricks
While I play on your 'collar' with sticks!
    Though my agent could shove it,
    Our audience would love it—
You'll sign paw-tographs and give licks!"

Though his plan was exceedingly clever,
He never succeeded, however;
    'Cause Fluff's head, though quite stout,

Of the "collar," slipped out—
And he shrugged and said, "Oh, well, whatever."

Yet their friendship began to cement,
'Cause wherever her master now went—
    Whether Rome or Peru—
    Little Fluffy went, too,
And now tough little Fluff is content!

(You can see on display in Nantucket,
A piece of that rusty, old bucket;
    It's in the town square,
    But it soon won't be there,
'Cause next week an official will chuck it.)

288
MY DOG'S DOGGINESS

A window on the vanishing wild,
By my dog I am often beguiled:
    While, with lupine-like skill,
    She stalks squirrels on the hill,
With my child, she's perfectly mild!

289
ADOPT ME PLEASE

Can you see I'm thrilled and happy that you came?
My tail is wagging. See? I'm very tame!
    And friendly, playful, loyal, brave;
    A home is all I truly crave,
So please adopt and then give me a name.

I'll protect you from all dangers that appear,
Such as squirrels, dogs, or muggers that come near.

But if they're friendly my big tail
Will wag a friendly greeting. They'll
See my body language loud and clear!

At dawn I'll wake you up with big, wet licks;
You'll throw big sticks, I'll fetch them just for kicks;
    We'll both have fun, we'll get some sun,
    Through fields and woods I'll romp and run,
And then with tweezers you can pick off ticks.

After breakfast and a nap I'll chase some deer;
Perhaps a fox or hare. But do not fear!
    For I'll always come when you will call.
    (I'll know my new name, after all.)
My ears, your voice from anywhere, will hear.

I'll then chase all the kitties all around;
And when I tire I'll be homeward bound.
    I'll come inside, take one more nap.
    A noise might make me bark and yap,
And then, I bet, you'll take me to the pound —

Which is where I am right now, as you can see;
For Heaven's sake, for me have empathy!
    For I really do not like this place!
    Can you not see my anxious face?
My life is not the way it used to be …

I had a master once. His name was Joe.
(His house from here is just a pebble's throw.)
    He got me when I was a pup,
    He played with me and picked me up,
But how to train me, Joe just didn't know.

He'd holler, bellow, clamor, yell, and roar.
I never could determine just what for.
    Round my neck he kept a chain;
    It sometimes choked me, gave me pain,
And then he started hitting more and more.

When I'd hear my master opening the door,
I'd tremble, shake, roll over on the floor.
    He'd shout and then my nose he'd smack
    Or kick me in the ribs or back—
It hurt my faithful heart right to the core!

I ran away one time, but I returned.
Why he punished me I never really learned.
    All I know is I was scared,
    And yet my teeth I never bared;
But in sleep I growled and yelped and tossed and turned.

He brought me to this place one cloudy day;
Then he left. I watched him go away.
    In this very cage they put me then;
    I can't recall exactly when,
But I will say that day was truly gray.

The day my master did his pup forgo
Feels like many melancholy moons ago.
    Don't walk away. Please don't say, "Nope!"
    With you, there's still a ray of hope.
With you, perhaps, I soon will get to go.

290
ROSS'S DOG

I know a young fellow named Ross
Who fed his dog warm applesauce.
    She also ate cake
    That her master did bake.
Now this doggy has major tooth loss!

The dog has lost all of her white
Teeth; she can no longer bite.
    Instead of big bones,

She got big ice cream cones.
('Bout some things Ross just wasn't too bright.)

The few times the poor mutt had a fight
With another dog, it was a sight!
    She never did win—
    When they'd see her big "grin,"
They would finish the quarrel outright!

But at Ross I just cannot be cross,
For he trained his good dog without force.
    He "clicked" and he treated
    And then he succeeded—
With positive methods, of course.

Though she's toothless, she's very well trained;
Some very high scores she's attained.
    In obedience tests
    She impresses the guests,
But from sweets the dog should have abstained!

Just yesterday I came across
That poor mutt and her kindhearted boss.
    She's not one single tooth,
    For when she was a youth,
Ross should have told her to floss!

291
A STRANGE MUTT

Have you heard of that mutt whose right paw
Is as large as a pelican's craw?
    He can open a door,
    He reads books on dog lore,
Writes poems, and with pencil can draw.

A picture he recently drew
Of a gnu in a zoo eating stew

With a spoon at high noon,
With a loon and baboon,
Is on view at the Whitney. It's true!

His drawings have been on display
In Norway, the States, and Bombay.
        He just recently sold
        A picture for gold
Of two two-headed pumas at play.

Though the pumas he drew are fictitious,
His drawing was very ambitious.
        (This dog cooks his own
        Lentil soup with a bone.
I've had it. It's very delicious!)

If you greet him your hand he will shake.
This strange dog you could never mistake
        For just any old cur
        Or mongrel. No sir!
With a knife he'll cut up his own steak!

'Cause his paw has four very large claws
And a "thumb" which will give people pause
        To watch and observe—
        Though the sight may unnerve
Unsuspecting observers like Roz.

Roz is my sister-in-law.
The first time that queer doggy she saw,
        She got so darn freaked out,
        She went pale and did shout—
A shriek like some big, mean macaw—

Which was really a normal reaction.
Yet it gave me a strange satisfaction,
        For the woman hates dogs—
        She thinks they're worse than frogs.
With dogs, she has no interaction.

That strange canine, who's black, brown, and white,
Writes strange poems in his doghouse at night.
    Completely nocturnal,
    He writes his infernal
Limericks by candlelight.

Most people, therefore, never see 'im.
When they do see 'im most people flee 'im.
    'Cause they can't stand the sight—
    His paw gives them a fright—
Yet they'll see his art in a museum.

Here is a typical rhyme
By this canine. It's truly sublime!:
    "O Molly, my Molly!
    You beautiful Collie,
Let's get together sometime!"

Here is another great poem
By the poet (composed in his home):
    "Many things I can tell
    From the smells that I smell
While the streets of my city I roam."

Though I've really just barely begun,
I will leave you with this final one,
    Which I think is the best
    Canine poem in the West—
Or perhaps even under the sun!

"Said Dog Dun to his dog friend, Dog Pun,
'Let's go for a run. 'Twill be fun!'
    Cried Dog Pun, 'Wait, not yet!
    For a hot dog I et,
But I haven't yet finished the bun!'"

292
FLASH

Down the street lives an Aussie named Flash
Who like lightning would go raid the trash.
    But she gained so much weight
    From the garbage she ate
She became quite self-conscious, abash.

In the dog shows they called her a laggard.
She could not even run. She felt haggard.
    She was so oversized
    She was quite criticized,
And at times the poor dog even staggered.

When she tried to leap over a jump
She could barely get off of her rump.
    She was no longer agile.
    Her mood was now fragile.
In gloom her poor spirit did slump.

Then one day she found the trash hid
In a can with a tight-fitting lid.
    Though Flash sure did try,
    She just couldn't pry
The lid off the can she made skid

Across the whole floor of the room.
(It even knocked over the broom.)
    She started to whine,
    Which was not a good sign,
But her mistress thought, *Go on and fume!*

I know what you're going through's rough,
But you're not eating garbage, so tough!
    You're gonna lose weight
    So you'll feel and look great,
And I'm sure you'll calm down soon enough.

Turns out the dog's mistress was right:
Though Flash didn't get slim overnight,
    She began to feel spryer,
    Jumped higher and higher,
And soon felt as light as a kite!

Then one day she swallowed a stone—
A lodestone that looked like a bone.
    Did it make the dog sick?
    No! The thing made her *quick*—
A quickness hitherto unknown.

With her mistress next day in the sun
She began a good four-mile run.
    Then like a gun shot,
    Flash sprinted. Great Scott!
And in four minute's flat she was done!

What I'm trying to tell you in rhyme
Is the Aussie made very good time.
    Four miles she ran
    In a four-minute span!
What's more, the dog stopped on a dime.

Next day the dog actually flew
In the sky (which was cloudless and blue).
    The owner, amazed,
    At her Aussie just gazed
Till Flash finally vanished from view.

They'd been playing an ordinary game.
Fetching Frisbees was Flash's main aim.
    The Frisbee sailed high.
    Flash leaped toward the sky,
And kept rising like smoke from a flame!

She had caught the white Frisbee all right,
Yet it seemed she would never alight.
    (Will Flash ever land

On grass or on sand?
Has a dog ever taken to flight?)

It appeared she would fly to the moon
In the light of that late afternoon.
    She had reached such a height
    That a lady, from fright,
Looking up at the Aussie, did swoon!

Flash's mistress thought, *This is a dream.*
When she pinched herself, it sure did seem
    She was still wide awake.
    Then she felt her heart break,
And big tears from her brown eyes did stream …

For just like a great bird of prey,
Her dog, in a flash, flew away.
    Flash did not understand,
    But the feeling was grand!
Folks will always remember the day

When she leaped for that Frisbee and soared,
And continued to rise and rise toward
    The heavens. By God!
    It was certainly odd.
A man watching thought, *Never, my Lord,*

Have I seen a dog jump into space!
Of the dog there was not any trace.
    "Superdog!" the man yelled.
    "That dog's unparalleled!"
Ten days later she landed with grace.

Flash held in her jaws a moon rock.
At the sight of it people did gawk.
    'Twas shiny but dark.
    Flash let out a bark.
The thing dropped and then shattered like chalk.

Flash's picture was now in the news.
Folks begged her to do interviews.

People gave her dog treats.
She met other athletes.
  (And her mistress made large revenues!)

Flash, who's now super athletic,
No longer looks rueful, pathetic.
    And not long ago
    She won Best in Show.
A celebrity, Flash is *MAGNETIC!*

(Last August an astronaut found
On the moon, in the dirt, near a mound,
    A white plastic disk.
    When the moonman did whisk
The thing up, he saw tooth marks! Profound!)

293
IF THEY ONLY KNEW!

When my neighbor, who's neighborly, walks 'er
Friendly and sociable Boxer,
    She cannot go two feet,
    Often falls on her her seat,
'Cause her dog gets in front and then blocks 'er.

When she walks round the block her spouse clocks 'er.
On returning, her husband then mocks 'er,
    'Cause two hours it takes 'er!
    For work that dog makes 'er
Late, and her manager docks 'er.

This dog has chased many a biker
And auto (but never a hiker).
    Although fond of the chase,
    She loves licking your face,
So there's no way you cannot but like 'er!

While her pugilistic boxer's mug
Will frighten a thief or a thug,
    The kids around here,
    Of the dog, have no fear.
They will pet her or give her a hug.

Since her tail had been docked very short,
When wagging she has to resort,
    Like that rocker named Elvis,
    To wag her whole pelvis —
She's an "in your face" sociable sort.

She's ugly but also a beauty.
She's strong but she's also a cutie.
    By herself she will stroll
    Round the block — thinks her goal
Is to guard all the houses: her duty.

Yet her owners know nothing about
Their dog's rounds she makes day in, day out.
    When the two are at work
    Their Boxer will smirk
And sneak off to walk her daily route.

When she gets to the very last house,
Out comes a fellow named Strauss,
    Who gives her a biscuit
    Or piece of a brisket.
(Or sometimes it's done by his spouse.)

Then she'll go back to her yard
Which, while her folks are working, she'll guard.
    When her masters come back,
    They give her a snack
And say, "Not that you've worked all that hard!

"While we have been toiling all day
Earning our bread and our pay,
    What have you done?

Just lain in the sun
Or the shade, in the yard or driveway!"

Near Strauss's house was a clock tower.
(The clock ran on electric power.)
    When, at various times,
    The dog heard its chimes,
She would cock her round head. It did wow 'er.

Though it wasn't apparent when seen,
The tower was starting to lean.
    (But the Boxer did sense
    Something odd and was tense,
For her senses are awfully keen.)

Each week the clock tower was tending
To lean more and more; it was bending.
    The chance was not small
    That the tower would fall.
The Boxer could sense doom impending.

Last week when she went for a walk
With her master around the whole block,
    She hurried right past
    Strauss's house fairly fast
For she knew she was under the clock!

The husband asked, "Did you guys run?
Or haven't you even begun?"
    Said the wife, "This here dog
    Pulled me into a jog."
Said the man to the Boxer, "Well done!"

The tower became very slanted.
In the ground it was not too well planted.
    The dog and her master
    Ran faster and faster—
Their speed was now taken for granted.

They were now so incredibly speedy,
So rapid, so swift, and so fleety,

They were quick as a bunny.
The man said, "Hey, honey,
   You really can run—yes, indeedy!"

Last Tuesday the clock tower fell.
Folks heard it as clear as a bell.
   Though no one was hurt,
   The dog did revert
To her habit of blocking—oh well!

(The Strausses were wondering why
For weeks the dog hadn't come by.
   But she now comes around
   Again—duty-bound—
With a rump-wag. She sure isn't shy!)

294
INDIGESTIBLE STUFF

There once was a sick Chinese Crested
Whose owner was nabbed and arrested.
   They said, "Next time think twice
   Before feeding her rice.
Don't you know that stuff can't be digested?"

Yet the master thought 'twas not the grain
That made his dog ill, but the rain,
   For a servant had let
   Her out in the wet,
Cold downpour—like a hurricane.

The dog had attempted in vain
To get in through her dog door again,
   But the dog door was stuck.
   The dog had no luck.
In the rain the dog had to remain.

As the storm moved away towards the east,
She shivered till wind and rain ceased.
    By this time 'twas dark.
    No one heard the dog bark
Till the din of the storm had decreased.

When at last she was let in the door,
The master was angry and sore.
    "Who let this dog out?"
    He asked with a shout.
"That person will work here no more!"

Then he fed his poor dog some chow mein
(With rice but no soy sauce—just plain).
    After having been fed,
    She went straight to her bed,
For she felt in her gut a sharp pain.

The dog, being hungry, did fill
Her stomach with rice and felt ill.
    She wasn't just faking—
    Her belly was aching.
She curled up in bed and lay still.

On the man someone called the police.
(Most likely it was the man's niece.)
    They came and they took him.
    The chief said, "Let's book him."
He knew not when they would him release.

The dog's master was now doing time
In jail for his terrible crime.
    While in jail he did stay,
    His dog pined away,
And was hoping the doorbell would chime.

But the dog soon recovered and went
To locate her master by scent—
    But not with *her* nose;

The nose that she chose
Was a Bloodhound's, who gave his consent.

His nose he had eagerly lent.
On the trail that big hound was hell-bent!
 His keen sense of smell
 Found the master's jail cell,
Where the man had spent days in torment.

Upon finding the master, the hound
Said, "Now that your master's been found,
 I will leave you alone.
 You're now on your own."
And walked off with his nose to the ground.

The Crested was seen by a guard.
At the door the dog's entrance was barred.
 So she bit the guard's toe
 'Cause she wanted to show
Him that though she is small, she bites hard!

Of that toe she just wouldn't let go.
The man's pain was beginning to grow.
 He pulled on her tail
 But to not much avail,
So he gave the dog's head a good blow.

She let go of her hold, and then scurried
Straight through the door. The dog hurried
 Faster and faster
 Right past her master,
Who saw her and yelled, "I was worried!"

She stopped in her tracks and whirled round,
Ran up to her man with a bound,
 And leaped into his arms,
 But the station's alarms
Were now blaring away—what a sound!

A guard ordered, "Put your hands up!"
Said the man, "But I'll then drop my pup."

Said the chief, "Listen, sir,
Your dog barely has fur.
She got sick from that rice in her sup!"

Said the master, "That's simply not true.
The hair on her skin never grew.
    You do not know the breed.
    It is true, I do feed
My dog rice, but she also gets stew.

"But she's no longer ill, as you see.
So why don't you just release me?"
    The chief said, "OK.
    There's the doorway.
Now beat it! Go on. You are free."

When the master got home the man fired
His niece, and next day he acquired
    A nice dog from the pound
    Which, though healthy and sound,
Upon eating a rice cake, expired!

295
ABANDONED

With chains they tied their dog up to a tree,
Moved out, and left poor Molly there to stay.
They went across the great, blue, wavy sea.
Away they sailed. They sailed far, far away.
Throughout the dreary day and somber night,
I heard the lonely Collie yelp and bark.
I knew something was odd, amiss, not right.
I walked across the way through gloomy dark.
No lights were on in house nor yard. But moon-
Light flickered off her keen but mournful eyes.
"You will not suffer any longer; soon
You'll be unchained. I'll no more hear your cries."

She watched me with a look so melancholy,
Forthwith I did unloose that lonesome Collie.
I took her home and gave her meat and bread
And water. Then she curled up on my bed
And dreamt that she slipped out through my back door,
And did what Collies do in canine lore: —
She went to search for her old family.
She crossed the great, blue sea where fish swim free.
Upon a giant turtle she did ride.
Her intuition was her only guide.
Smart Molly brought with her fresh water in
A bottle, hung from the sea turtle's chin.
The turtle's friend, a dolphin, caught much fish
Which he'd present to Molly on a dish.
So Molly had enough to drink and eat.
(She started liking fish much more than meat.)
Under blue sky, on tranquil salty ocean,
The dog and turtle felt the gentle motion
Of waves and currents rocking to and fro.
The zephyr from the west did gently blow.
So far the boundless water felt quite warm;
Yet in the distance they did sense a storm.
Dark clouds began to roll in from the east.
The waves grew large. The wind had now increased.
And soon a fierce, torrential rain came down
Upon their heads and Molly feared she'd drown.
The wind was violent now — a hurricane —
Too much for Collie, Newfie, or Great Dane!
The waves seemed like they were a mile high!
And lightning bolts came crashing from the sky!
She hung on for dear life. For if she'd slipped
Off that great turtle, she was not equipped
To float. (She was not wearing a life vest.)
On that great reptile's back she did her best,
With all her canine energy and might
To straddle its huge shell. She hung on tight!
She hoped and prayed they would not now capsize.
("Turn turtle" is a phrase which now applies.)
The storm had lasted all the night and day,

But slowly, very slowly, moved away.
The sky was once again deep azure blue.
The coast, a hazy hue, was now in view.
Her longing and her yearning greatly grew,
For there is where her folks are. (She just knew.)
When finally they reached that distant shore,
She thanked the turtle, then went to explore:
Trotting o'er hill and dale, through woods and plain,
Crossing great rivers, mountains, fields of grain.
Her paws were bleeding. Barely they had skin.
Her fur was matted. She was gaunt and thin —
For she had journeyed over much terrain.
(It would have been much speedier by train!)
Worn-out by now, she ran a turtle's pace,
Yet still their whereabouts she tried to trace.
Though she was in much agony and pain,
She knew in time she would her goal attain.
(This wasn't just a silly wild-goose chase.)
Five hundred miles inland she found their place!
She saw them walking down the boulevard,
But ran ahead and waited in their yard.
She watched them coming near and panting hard,
Now towards her former masters she did race.
Wagging her tail, expecting an embrace,
She suddenly woke up and licked my face!
And with a bound ran out the doorway then —
And never did I see that dog again!

296
THE DOG AND I

I often dog-sit for my neighbor, Sue.
Her dog sticks by my side like super glue.
Fluff likes me more than he likes her. It's true!

Though to his owner it does not seem fair,
Fluff's not content unless he's in my care.
We're buddies. We are pals. We are a pair.

For looking after Fluff I want no present
Or money, for the job is rather pleasant
(Except the times he chased a deer or pheasant).

The dog and I walked to the reservoir
One day. From our place it was pretty far.
We walked, for I did not then have a car.

Mid-afternoon was when we started out.
The dog, a mid-sized mongrel, with his snout,
Began at once to nose and sniff about.

But just a few blocks later we walked straight,
And then maintained a fairly rapid rate.
(Though when we left, it was a bit too late.)

A splendid autumn day it was that day.
Under the azure sky we made our way
Towards the reservoir without delay.

We strode past many houses, trees, and scores
Of stores where folks went in and out of doors.
There aren't too many folks that dog ignores;

When folks approach, the dog will wag his tail—
'Specially mailmen with or without mail.
(The post office gives cookies without fail.)

The avenue has lots of traffic noise:
The ambulances my poor ear annoys,
And motorcycles Fluffy's ear destroys.

Yet Fluff (which Sue adopted from the pound)
Took hardly any notice of the sound
Of traffic while with me he walked around.

Though he will sometimes bark at rumbling trucks,
Where we were headed, there are geese and ducks
And squirrels and owls and chipmunks and woodchucks.

The dog and I were walking really fast.
Dozens of people and some dogs we'd passed.
Just up ahead we saw the forest, vast!

About two hours of walking we had done.
(We mostly walk. We hardly ever run.)
In front of us we saw the setting sun.

Behind us towards the east was the full moon.
And though we'd reach our destination soon,
I wished we'd started out at least by noon;

For by the time we reach the woodsy trail
The light will quickly fade — it will be pale —
And our adventure in the woods curtail.

But all the same I took the dog in there.
The weather for this time of year was fair,
And we enjoyed the cool foresty air.

While we were walking happy as a lark,
I knew it was forbidden after dark
To run or hike or bike inside the park;

But we were having fun, for I could see
Enough to keep on walking. I felt free.
What's "dark" is just a matter of degree.

The dog can see in dusk better than me,
So he can guide me clear of any tree.
When hiking we're a team — that is the key.

When I am with this dog I do not fear
The creatures of the night, for he can hear
When bear or bird or fox or deer comes near.

We just had left the park — 'twas now nightfall —
When suddenly I heard a man's voice call,
With words quite clear and crisp (no drawl at all),

"Come up here, I'm a police officer.
You need to come back up here right now, sir.
Put up your hands!" So I said, "OK, sure."

The path we'd just gone down leads to a street
Beyond the park. We now were fifty feet
Below the man who'd better not mistreat

Me or the dog! I raised my hands and said,
"I have a good attorney!" I did dread
That stranger, for he could just shoot us dead!

His searchlight aimed directly at my face,
We climbed back up. Our steps we did retrace.
I kept both of my hands up (just in case).

I told him I can't see were I am going,
'Cause straight into my eyes his light was glowing.
My fear and anger now was greatly growing!

I was surprised when he turned off the light,
Which really in my eyes was very bright.
But now they readjusted to the night.

When Fluff and I had reached the top, I was
Immediately questioned by the fuzz.
I asked him why and then he said, "Becuz

"A fellow with a knife had come inside
The park today to commit suicide."
(The dog was all this time by my left side.)

He searched me, held my hands behind my back,
And handcuffed me, and went through my backpack.
Dog treats and water he found in the sack.

But that was all he found. There was no knife.
I said, "Though in my life there is some strife,
I did not come in here to take my life."

While I stood on my feet which now felt tired,
Next to me stood the dog whom I admired.
And next to us, in uniform attired,

The cop heard on his police radio,
"The suspect is about eighteen, you know.
He's on a bike." The officer said, "Oh!

"Well, maybe this guy here had ditched the bike."
(And then picked up a dog with which to hike?)
That officer I really didn't like!

After a while two more cops then came.
One shone a light in my poor eyes. (Good aim!)
He said, "That isn't him!" (What was their game?)

"You have no ID on you. That's the reason
We held you here. It just was not us pleasin'."
(It now was getting cold. I started freezin'.)

One of them took the handcuffs off at last.
Yet I could not but feel I'd been harassed.
But then what happened next made me aghast:

One cop came close, crouched low, and said, "Now what
Is this dog, sir, a pure breed or a mutt?"
(Fluff wagged his tail, his pelvis, his whole butt!)

He said, "Does your dog bite?" I said, "Why, no."
"Oh, God!" he screamed. "Your dog bit my elbow!"
"That's not my dog!" said I. "Now may I go?"

Forthwith they threw the two of us in jail.
I didn't have one cent on me for bail.
('Twas there that I'd begun to write this tale.)

Fluff's pawprints and my fingerprints they took,
And then our mug shots they took for their book.
Though I was just a schnook, I'm now a crook!

They put us in a cell all to our own.
I'm glad I'm here with Fluff and not alone.
They even threw the dog a meaty bone!

The bed which Fluff sleeps on is really swell!
It's stuffed with cedar shavings. It does smell
Like cedar. Fluffy likes it. You can tell.

(The bed *I* sleep on's narrow, hard, and small.
My feet hang off, and I'm not even tall!)
They also gave the dog a Jolly Ball.

But we've not one small window for a view.
You can't tell if the sky is gray or blue
Or red or green or any other hue.

And there's a man in an adjacent cell
Who babbles day and night. This man will dwell
On all his problems, and he does it well!

The fare here's fairly foul I hate to say
(And I'm not all that fussy — no gourmet).
Most of my meals to Fluff I give away.

Though I am fasting, Fluff gets a buffet!
But we do lots of training and we play.
(Yet when I lie in bed I often pray.)

The dog, last Monday, licked the warden's face.
They took him home. He's at his owner's place.
But I still sit here waiting for my case …

It's been three weeks now. What am I to do?
It seems to me my trial's overdue.
I'm starting now to fret and mope and stew.

At last this morning in a court of law
The judge determined it was Fluffy's claw
That scratched the cop when he held out his paw!

I'm finally at home and feeling glad.
That was quite an adventure I had had!
I'm looking after Fluff, my good comrade.

We're in a bank now on the boulevard.
Fluff's wagging his entire … But the guard
Says, "Does he bite?" I glared at that man hard!

297
THE DOG AND THE FLY

The dog said, "I will catch you, you black fly!"
"I dare you!" said the fly. "I'm mighty quick!"
The dog jumped up so fast and so darn high,
He looked like he was on a pogo stick.
"Did you think you could take me by surprise?
Not even close!" the fly laughed. "I'm too fast!"
The dog said, "Almost caught you on the rise.
The next time you will not my teeth fly past!"

The fly then buzzed around a little more,
And pondered her agility and speed.
Yet soon a dreadful fate did lie in store
For that poor fly. God did not intercede.
When briefly on a web she did alight,
That fly received a lethal spider's bite!

298
THINK I'LL SLEEP ON THE COUCH TONIGHT

He rolled on something super smelly—
   'Twas for three days dead;
And then with horse dung filled his belly—
   Now he's on my bed!

299
A FEW HAIKU FOR YOU

First you ate horse dung.
Then you rolled on a dead frog.
Now you want a hug?

My dog does no work.
Then why do I feed the mutt?
He's good company.

As I scratched his chest,
The dog's hind leg tried its best
To give me a hand.

My dog makes me walk
Every day in rain or shine.
That's worth his kibble.

Stars shine bright tonight;
Yet the love in my dog's eyes
Is brighter by far!

My friend has a car.
My dog likes him more than me.
I make my dog walk.

I know cool dog tricks,
But I don't do them for kicks—
Only for cookies.

My master said, "Fetch!"
But the ball is in the lake.
It's over my head!

I rub your belly.
You look up and lick my face.
You smell like a skunk.

My dogs often play,
Sometimes they fight, and sometimes
They do both at once.

I'll come when you call
If you have those tasty treats.
If not—forget it!

It is my nature
To chase squirrels, mice, rats, and cats—
Yet you restrain me.

The dog was begging.
I held garlic near his nose.
He drew back a step.

"Roll over, Rover!"
He knows how, but won't right now;
My pocket's empty.

The opossum fled.
You caught up and found her "dead."
Once more she fooled you.

You deigned not to pee
On that giant redwood tree;
My leg looked better.

The pup bit my hand.
His sharp, little teeth left marks.
"Woof!" was his remark.

The pup chewed my shoe.
I did not yell, "Shame on you!"
I gave her a toy.

You have to stop now
To sniff, pee, and scratch the ground?
Well, I'll jog in place.

The shy, horny dog
Tries to mount even a log,
But only in fog.

What dog does not bark,
Beg, drool, jump, chase cars, or shed?
The stuffed one in Ames.

300
MY DOG'S JAWS

It's quite plain, from the bones that she gnaws,
My sweet Molly has murderer's jaws.
    Skunk, raccoon, or opossum —
    If she comes across 'em …
Well, I'll just observe the leash laws!

301
FLAGRANTLY FRAGRANT

I think that my dog's greatest wish
Is to roll on a smelly, dead fish.
    He also likes mice,
    But I don't think it's nice
When the creature he rolls on goes "squish!"

302
MY SINGING BASENJI

My Basenji does not, of course, bark,
But she sings just as well as a lark.
    A coloratura
    Who sang with bravura,
In the opera world, she left her mark.

She sang twelve different operas a year,
And was known for her excellent ear.
    Her pitch was so sure
    And her tone was so pure
That her listeners, enthralled, would all cheer!

Her voice, loud and clear as a bell,
Transfixed you and caused tears to swell.
    Her voice never cracked.
    The theaters were packed.
All were awed till the last curtain fell.

Her fan club consisted of bats,
Opossums, raccoons, mice, and rats,
    Badgers, beavers, and bears,
    Humans, horses, and hares,
Coyotes ... and even some cats.

Then one evening while singing Menotti,
At the Met with the great Pavarotti,
    In the opening scene
    Something quite unforeseen—
Without warning, the dog made a potty

Right on the proscenium stage!
The director went into a rage.
    The orchestra stopped,
    The curtain then dropped,
And they put the poor dog in a cage.

That was it for my doggy's career.
But she still loves to sing, never fear!
    Though she can't go, "Bow wow,"
    The good Lord did endow
Her with a voice that is pure crystal clear!

Of late she sings oldies and folk
And jazz. (Do you think I would joke?)
    She's now singing for me
    With her paw on my knee
As we sit in our yard by the oak.

303
I KNOW NONE

Whereas some love to doze in the sun,
And others just *fly* when they run;
    What *all* canines do
    Is be loyal to you.
I know none that are not—not a *one!*

304
DOGMA

Among all the dogs under the sun,
I'm most common, yet no other one
    Is like me. I'm unique —
    In physique, *magnifique!*
I'm a mutt, and I'm second to none!

305
COYOTE QUATRAINS

Coyotes howling in the night —
    What do their cries suggest?
Do they give you a tingly fright,
    Or remind you of the West?

C. *latrans* is their Latin name,
    Which means the "barking dog."
Small "prairie wolves" they are — not tame
    Like your pet dog or hog.

They look just like a little Collie;
    Bushy tail is round.
When frolicking they sure are jolly!
    Twirl and leap and bound.

Evasive, stealthy, swift, and sly,
    With senses super keen,
You'll rarely glimpse one running by,
    For they are seldom seen.

Small desert dogs don't weigh that much.
    Their fur's light gray or tan.
But larger mountain dogs have such
    Nice fur, they're trapped by man.

They play in nature a vital role
    Like wolves and jackals do.
Each day they'll eat a mole or vole,
    Perhaps a hare or two,

Ground squirrels, insects, reptiles, fruit,
    Or fish, or food that's spoiled.
But sometimes sheep. Then farmers shoot
    Those dogs with guns well oiled.

Yet coyotes do not harm your farm;
    They help by catching mice.
So if you wish those dogs to harm,
    You really should think twice!

Those canines catch small creatures that
    Most folks consider vermin.
Each time *C. latrans* eats a rat,
    He is my point confirmin'.

Because they're less than wolves in size
    And need less meat to eat,
Despite how human hatred tries,
    It can't these dogs defeat!

Most wolves are gone from this great land
    We call the USA.
Coyotes, though, increase, expand
    Their range — they're here to stay!

306
CODA (TAIL)

Since ignoring your dog is a crime,
With great speed you must read this last rhyme!
    For he may stray away!
    If you want him to stay,
With your dog spend some quality time!

Did you have, with these rhymes, any fun?
I sure hope so! But now that you're done,
    Go get your dog's ball,
    Then your dog go and call,
And go out and play fetch in the sun!

CLOSING CANINE COUPLETS

Dogs are very cool I'd say,
For all they want to do is play;
To run, have fun, lay in the sun.
In play, dogs cannot be outdone!
Their nose and ears are super keen;
Their eyes can make out things (unseen
By ours) that move in dim twilight:
Nocturnal creatures of the night.
Some dogs come when we do call;
Some dogs love to fetch a ball;
Some are keen at learning tricks;
Others simply chew on sticks.
Some just want to lick your face;
Others simply want a place
In your kind heart — that's all they ask.
(Though working dogs just want a task.)
All want a place to lay their head:
A dog bed (or perhaps *your* bed);
Some food, some water, some shelter,
So rain or snow won't wet their fur.
You need not be cold in a winter's storm;
If you've a dog, he'll keep you warm.
But more than that, your dog's your friend —
Loyal to the very end.
Since dogs don't care for separation,
When we leave for our vocation
For three hours, never fear,
They'll greet us like it's been a year!
For at least ten thousand years or so
We've been with canines. Did you know?
They've worked for us in many ways —
Like tending sheep (still do these days);

They helped us humans hunt for meat
With stealth and skill and agile feet.
Without a doubt they've helped us out
(Yet some folks clout their good dog's snout).
At least four hundred canine breeds
Were made by us for our own needs:
The giants and the dwarfs, the freaks,
They're canines all — none yet have beaks.
In numbers, mongrels beat them all,
Yet all dogs, whether large or small,
Or mutts or pure breeds need us folk.
If not for us, they'd all just croak!
Or maybe not — perhaps *we* would,
For dogs do much for us that's good!
A symbiotic thing we've got
With Fido, Rover, Sam, or Spot.
They guard, pull sleds, they herd livestock;
They lead the blind around the block.
But mostly they're good company;
With us, most dogs just love to be.
If not for dogs, we might not be
Here now today — not you nor me!
Let's keep our bond, we women and men,
With our true friend, the dog. Amen!

AFTERWORD

I've been so absorbed in putting the finishing touches on this book that of late, I've been guilty of neglecting my motley mutts. I had better go see what the rascals are up to ... Oh, there they are, waiting by the front door.

"Do you have to go out?"

"Yes, Marty.

> "We've waited very patiently
> While you worked on your poetry;
> Now that you're finished, finally,
> Please let us out. We need to pee!"

Well, it's time for a walk. Adiós! Or should I say *woof?*

ACKNOWLEDGMENTS

If not for my two great canines,
I would never have written these lines.
    My gratitude goes,
    Not only to those,
But to dogs everywhere of all kinds.

Now for those humans who were there
    To give me feedback when
I was still trying to prepare
    This book with my own pen:

Beverly and Marshal Brown,
Who live a stone's throw from my town;
Lynette and Dave Giardina and
Frank Guarco—they were truly grand!
Betty Liebman was for me
Helpful to a high degree;
Joan (who plays the harp) Ceo
Was most enthusiastic. Oh!
And Fran Vanasco from New York
Helped fine tune words like a tuning fork!

Suzanne Haws I wish to thank as well
    For copyediting,
And her book design turned out so swell
    It made me want to sing!

Caninically yours,

Martin Elster

INDEX OF TITLES

Index of First Lines

John Simpson, a Confederate spy, 66
Kibble is quite a bland diet, 242
Kneeing your dog in the chest, 150
More efficient than any machine, 37
Muscles taut, tail is held high?, 127
My Basenji does not, of course, bark, 302
My Beagle's been chasing this rabbit, 70
My Corgi, on cue, will "roll over," 211
My corpulent mutt who's aloof, 159
My dog is a horrible beast!, 142
My dog is a warm-blooded creature, 126
My dog is now controlling, 1
My dog is so clever and smart, 35
My dog just got sprayed by a skunk!, 12
My dog loves to go ride in the car, 41
My dog rolls on objects so rotten, 280
My dog saw a blimp in the sky, 264
My dog, sound asleep, softly snoring, 172
My dog's done some mischievous stunts, 231
My dog's ears just perked up from a sound, 209
My friend gave my pup something hot, 153
My friend who arrived from Hong Kong, 214
My guide dog is truly a must, 234
My intelligent Rhodesian Ridge, 170
My large, lanky mongrel named Sonya, 206
My nine-month-old Rottie was naughty, 116
My parents were constantly fighting, 93
My pooches won't swim in the ocean, 16

My puppy just grabbed a pig's ear, 216
No dogs allowed in this place, 218
Objects for me imperceptible, 149
Of good garbage there's rarely a lack, 252
Okay is a good release word, 117
On cue my Dalmatian will spin, 259
On his hind legs my doggy will stand, 38
On our way to obedience class, 17
One of my dogs loves a carrot, 87
Perhaps more than a husband or wife, 90
Perhaps the word *dog* in reverse, 188
Pesticides they want to test, 174
Pit Bulls are nice until taught, 148
Poodles sure do love the water!, 121
Scott's giant Newfie named Spot, 113
Shock me again and I'll bite!, 160
Shows are for dogs that have money, 233
Siblings Wally and Ollie and Polly, 32
Since ignoring your dog is a crime, 306
Sometimes my dogs make me mad, 71
Spike is a dog that I like, 286
That guy's lawn mower sure makes some noise!, 235
The dog had just ruined the Seder!, 253
The dog ran too fast for his master, 10
The dog said, "I will catch you, you black fly!", 297
The doggy came out of the brook, 123
The farmer was turning his back, 228
The man dogged us down the side walk, 217

INDEX OF BREEDS

ABOUT THE AUTHOR

Martin Elster is a guy with two dogs. He is also a percussionist with the Hartford Symphony Orchestra and the Connecticut Opera Association Orchestra, as well as a published composer.

Printed in the United States
21769LVS00003B/52-57